House of Mirrors

Poems

Józef Tracz-Ripple

Copyright © 2015 Józef Tracz-Ripple
& Multiverse Books

Front Cover Art: Original Artwork by Hassan Musa Copyright © 2015

Back Cover Art: Metatron's Cube, "The Fruit of Life," Creative Commons & Multiverse Books Insignia Copyright © 2015

All rights reserved.

ISBN: 0692471081
ISBN-13: 978-0692471081

with infinite Love:
for the Friend, all of my loves,
and my babcia i dziadek.

CONTENTS

	Acknowledgments	i
	Author's Notes	ii
1	The Mystery	1
2	Dying	44
3	Light	75
4	Polishing	97
5	Stories	118
6	Friendship	151
7	Laughing	180

ACKNOWLEDGMENTS

Words are incomplete, but we must. My gratitude is uncontainable for all my dearest friends and loves, my brothers and sisters, and everyone I have met along the path or inside the Tavern, who have supported me and inspired me with their beautiful souls. For all the tragedy and suffering, for all the love and joy, these are petals on the same flower, growing from a single root. Let your root be love, not fear. Dissolve from self into Light. For awareness and understanding and compassion, I am forever in debt to all of you for these gifts: You have lain jewels at my feet when I was a beggar with a broken bowl. You made me beautiful when all I felt was ugliness. You loved me when I was convinced I was unloveable. You grasped my hand and dragged me from darkness into Light.

AUTHOR'S NOTE

Words and compassion, given to me, have been the wind through the weathervane of my soul. The thoughts and feelings given to me, this wind, have set me in the right direction. This is Love's power. It craves our powerlessness. Despite common thinking, distance or absence can unlock hope, love, revelation, beauty, safety, sanctuary, and an infinite amount of things filled with both wonder and majesty. Any ship lost in the eternal nighttime of the sea, when glancing upon the beacon of The Lighthouse that guides them, becomes unburdened from the worry and released with the relief: they know they are coming Home.

THE MYSTERY:

*

And I'll never know:
were the birds flying
or were they leaves
heaved into
the autumnal air?

*

Who owns
this magnificent
Garden
of the Soul?

*

i am the future
i am the worshipper
of the wind and streams
of the trees and autumn leaves
of the coyote, of the bee,
of solemn truth & eternity.

My blood is yours.
It is running through me
like a calm breeze.

The night is the gnawer of bones.
Your love: my temple,
my holy home.

*

What is the source of this mist,
these hollowed sounds?
They are the paint on canvas.
They are voice in my mouth.
The blood on analog tapes.
The shaman's dream-talk:
Music.

*

We find ourselves,
star-strewn and chapped-lipped,
desert wanderers,
sucklings of date seeds,
standing face-ward
at the sea's shoreline
once again.

*

i am a dead leaf
that refuses
to unhang
from the tree.

Pluck me
from the grasp
and pull me apart.

Toss me into the fire
and watch me
flutter into the sky.

*

The invisible tongue,
buried at the foot
of a cypress tree
in the rose garden
of Shiraz.

Pile up like
dirt underneath
my fingernails.

Fill my mouth
with the wine;
i am drunk off
the poetry
of your Heavenlips
again, aren't i?

*

Every godloved word
of every godloved poem
of every godloved song,
i have stolen...

But godspeed
and bonne chance!
to those
seeking the thread
in this darkness.

Cause in lightness,
laughter, and dance,
with the leafed branch,
i brush the snow
and cover my tracks
oh so well.

But at least now,
the truth
you know.

*

What am *i* ?
A poet, you say?
i laugh.
A philosopher?
double-nay!

a blatherer
a ranter
a madman
a seamster

a screamer
a laugher
a fool
with illumined spool

i am simply
an Aeolian Harp,
designed with perfection
beyond my own hands.

The Wind just blows through me.

*

Oh dear God,
you must
really think
us poets
are your
bastard children!
And we are.
Always picking your pockets,
to give and give and give…

*

Fuck,
i have run out of
stone tablets again.

So look closely,
cause now i am just
writing words for you
on the tree leaves
and upon the clouded sky.

*

i can't even breathe
without songs coming out.

i can't even open my mouth
without all my teeth becoming poems.

*

Now i am just deliberately
kicking over all
the building blocks
and spilling the soup
all over the floor.

These poems shouldn't
assemble themselves so easily.

*

Yes, i get it now.
My mouth is not my own.
i sing for you and you alone.

But you've blessed me
the owner of my self,
now let me kiss that dear angel,
my speckled bird, right on her mouth!

*

My words,
they flow from prophet mouths.
They are not my own.

i am an illusion.

The only thing that is real
is this sea of suffering
of all my brothers and sisters
that my heart breathes
through my body and bones.

Even saviors
need saving.

*

Where do my poems
emerge from, you may ask?

i ask my Beloved for a Kiss,
and press these Lips to Her,
and while my eyes are closed,
She stuffs Pomegranate Flowers
and Date Seeds in my pockets
for me to
find
later.

*

i don't need a response.

i feel you in my marrow
and my abysmal heart.

i will write for you
forever, regardless.

*

And if you didn't get it,
perhaps you've been
reading them all wrong.

Yes, i've been stealing,
but i have been
plaguerizing
this entire time.

And i sincerely hope
you catch what i'm spreading.

*

Ha! The Joke!

i didn't even
open my mouth
this time.

And i misspoke.

*

Parthenogenesis:

Yusuf talks of the platonic form.

How She is Nature's fractal growth,
dendritic and reaching.
More perfect than the Fibonacci
sunflower, cacti, and pinecone...

Jeez! My head is spiraling,
every time i find the Universe
hidden in your eyes.

*

When will i stop
writing for you?
When i stop
breathing for you.

Even then,
this earth will still
see my heaven poems...

They'll be the shooting stars.
The songbird's morning call.
The sun removing
its shy face from clouds
to warm your body like i once did.

In all things:
of You,
i'll always sing.

*

Mashuq! Mashuq!
Come ring
my doorbell!
Your symphony
has been
panging around
in my heart chambers
for centuries now.

*

You were the Greatest Shout.
A thunderclap, rolling over
all the meadows and mountains
hidden inside of me.
Dark caverns that i never
knew existed. Absent-minded
ignorance to the fact
that i am but a hollow chamber.

Until you. Until you sang
and bellowed breath into me
to teach me, to show me.
Until. You.

*

Unrequited Love Letters:

i am your Aeolian Harp.
You are my Wind.

i miss you.
i am nothing. i can sing not,
without you.

Come back to me.

*

Hair like trees!
Oh wind,
dance with me.
Kiss me! Kiss me!

*

Kiss me
with your
smoky breath.

There are
pyres burning
of love
inside of
me also.

*

i have no pen.
Only a body full of blood.
i pull all my words
from the wind.
Thankfully, it's quite
windy up here on
this mountain top.
My blood blows like
rain, covering the trees
and filling the streams.
Everything is one with me.

*

i carry Mountains
and Caves in my front pocket.
Come out Prophetess.
Come stay with me.

*

Beautiful Bird,
let my Light
and my Love
into your heart

So i can sing
through your mouth.

*

How many holy funeral pyres
have i lain upon for you?

Not nearly enough,
oh, Bright Star'd One!

i am burning luminously.
The ice is all dripping.

Eternal spring is coming.
It is at your fingertips.

*

Deep down i'm really
just a stupid simpleton.
God just happened to leave
Her purse loose,
and a big, beautiful Gem
fell out of it and landed
in the worthless
turd
that
i am.

*

i have more love
hidden like dirt
under one fingernail
than any other
person could
ever try to give.

And this is for you for free.
There's no price
you must pay for it.

i only left my solitude home,
as the mountain-covered mist,
to climb the labyrinth ladder
into your heart with a Kiss.

*

i've been practicing,
putting the fire
to my lips and
breathing it in
to burn my lungs.

Because i know when
you finally kiss me,
i will turn
completely
into ash.

*

i was a barren tree
with no leaves.

Then, you came to me.

Now i am full bloom'd,
breathing the life of spring.

*

i stopped eating,
so i'm sucking on date seeds
and walking through
the Desert of your Love,
looking for your oasis
to wet my lips
with the knowledge
of everything. Like a prophet,
you took from me
the deepest love
in my world,
and i've wandered
in darkness, finding
pearls hidden in the
wells and caves of myself.
Alms of Lightness.
The shirts on my back
torn from behind
from the eager palms of women,
like Yossef, i've come here
wayfarer and wanderer.

For exactly two decades,
aimlessly i've floated on your
sea like driftwood,

tangled in currents
and riddled with soul-bruises.

And then the sun shined
through the tiniest of cracks
in my hidden chamber
to guide me, You guided me!

Out of the illusion,
out from the ephemeral night.
Eyes trained for years,
unblinded by the final light.

*

Fuck you! i *love* you!
i am made of everything.
i am older than every grain and stone.

So heave 10 billion millstones
upon my holy corpse. Watch
me still emerge from the raging sea!

With a delicate brush of my smallest
painter's finger, i will dispel
Sisyphus's boulder into the abyss
to be a bridge for all my brothers and
sisters, and i'll kiss that tired old
bastard's face!

Chain me along the cove stones!
And i'll uplift those Promethean bones!
And my dear brother, the Crow!
Eat of me, if you are hungry.
For i shall feed you!

What is eternity
to the man in me,
who is eternal
himself?

What is suffering
to the woman in me,
who is nature's living
maternal grace?

*

There are meadows
of flowers blooming
from my chest,
and She paints inside
of me, all vibrant
beautiful colors.

*

Welcome to my Heart!
Please be sure not
to keep your hands
and legs inside the
vehicle as it's moving.
Create all kinds of ruckus.
Do as much vandalism
as you'd like. Be truly you,
who you most truly are.

You are safe in here.
i love You.

*

i am a slow-growing Lotus,
where i've spent most
of my life, tangled in Mud,
drowning in dark cold
waters, reaching reaching...

But i've tread this water
for centuries now, and i've
eaten all the Suffering
that this Pond of the Universe
has to offer. And finally,
finally i've bloomed from
the water's beautiful Face,
so much like your own.

i've sprung out, singing
and blowing kisses to You,
basking in your unbelievable Light.

*

The best advice i could
ever give you is this:
please stay far away from me.
i am all of the blinding Light.
But there is a whispering
plague that follows me.
i dance joyfully,
simply so i am
always one clever step ahead.

My Light can touch you from
anywhere below or beyond Stars.

*

Oh, how great is the great Mystery!
It only gets greater as we age!
And you weigh down on me
like a billion rain clouds.
Heavier than my heart, you can be!
But lighter than the last breath!
Turn me back to dust!
Lift all of us back up!

*

All *i am* is your candlelight!
i burst to flame with your Touch
or am blown out with your Breath.

i pass through phases of existence
and nonexistence more casually
than the seasons with your Will.

Let me dance illumination upon
your seraphim smile a little
longer in this darkness, or let
me fade out cause i've got a secret:

just like the Great I,
fire will never die!

*

i've crept through the twilight
with my faint Moon Mistress
guarding my back on my
perfect mission. To you
i've wandered towards

like light in delicate reverence
through ancient geometric
domes of such sacredness
our world now hardly know.

i've followed the fine dress
and tails of that Light breaking
my body through all the darkness
and dancing in the Moonlight.

My path had only one end
on this perfect mission.
My cupped hands carried
for epochs my swollen jewel
of this and all Worlds.

i buried it at your favorite tree
while you slept. i buried it at
your birdsong feet, so pleasant
and so sweet.

It was my heart,
beating now in the dirt,
sending Love and Life and Light
into the world that surrounds you.
It's true. My only heart.
But shhh, it's for only You.

*

Oh tears of joy!
Tears of surrender!
What a great Fire
and great Mystery
you've alighted

in such a beautiful
mind, bestowed
like dowry gold!

*

You are an Invisible
Bridge hidden in Fog.
How i found you,
i'll never truly know.
But i turn my feet
into lips and kiss
You with every
step as i go.

*

Most days
i try.
i try so fucking hard
not to get locked
away in an insane asylum.

So i speak very little
in public, or just of
casual banterings.

Lord have mercy
if i were to really
say something...
out there!

*

Deep in your Irises,
i watch the Cherry
Blossoms bloom
and the petals
fall in Spirals to
the soft Earth.

*

Sleeping next to me,
you wake slightly
and your mouth
cracks open to yawn:
i watch Rosebushes
come pouring out.
And to be truthful,
which i can only
be to you, my love,
i am not surprised
at all by your Miracles.

*

How many Roses
must be planted
in my Garden
before i can
attract the
only Bird
i want?

How many Songs
must be sung
under the Moon's
orb'd Glow

in order to make
the Heavenflower grow?

And the only Tyger
of my darkest night,
burn burn burning so Bright.

Let these useless words
plant more Seeds
than i could ever know.

Her Love is the only
Gift that at my end
i wish to show.

*

i feel you deeply
in the Wind's touch,
incapable of grasping you.
i try to understand.
Enamored hearts
know the deepest longing,
arching towards the Light's source,
Forgiveness and Compassion
singing their thronging.

Tonight is my last night on earth,
so know my final truth:
Your lips on mine were
my greatest achievement.
Your mind and soul
were the only perfection
and comfort i ever found
or had in this life.

*

Love Notes:

My Princess, my Majesty!
i miss so much your
sweet caresses, and your
heavenly Kisses blowing
against my meager flesh.
i'll wait here for you
for as long as i must!
For i know you shall return!
-Weathervane

*

Oh, Yusuf!
You holy bastard bard!
You condemned angel
with weathered wings!
You Black Bird!
Push your Stones.
Sow your Seeds.
Never stop weaving
Gold in the Sunlight
above that Sweet Bird's
Crown. Never let us down!

Do you not see
all the blessings
that follow the Storms?

The Rain bows in the Sky
above the Princess's feet!
and so do you!

*

That time Maryem and Youssef
sat within a cube:
we talked of Joseph's tale.
His clothes torn because
of his great coveted Beauty.
You wrote my name down,
from right to left.
The resonant vibration
of every Sound and Syllable.
i watched your hand move
like a seismograph along the paper.
"You are a blackbird," she said.

*

City of Whispers
where the Wolves
are kissing instead
of just licking their Lips.

Where there are Crowns
of Laurel and Hyacinth
rather than tangled Thorns.

Where all your Roses
sprout themselves from
all the fresh soil of my soul,
and the Birds are cheering you on.

*

For decades,
women have prostrated
themselves at my feet.
i cannot articulate what sorts
of confusion this has arisen in me.

i am the Light and the Wind,
the Ungraspable. Your deepest
Love, calling to you always.
i am no thing. i am everything,
i am all that flows within.
That holy temple of your Flesh.
i am the humming in your Heart.
i am the vibration in your Blood.
i am the culmination of your Soul.

i am no one.
no one but You.
i am so glad
you've learned
to love Yourself.

i've always been here for you.

*

Did you make the Angel
return to her hiding place,
because of my silly desires?
The want of knowing the Touch
of her flesh. Her fingertips upon me.
Or my want of knowing her Taste
from above her chin
and below her waist?
But you know i see deep

beyond such silly sensations.
When i Look, i peer deep
under all the layers like
a Grand Excavator.
i lower my Bucket of Light into
the abyss and find the treasures.
i find the Mirror, and long
for the Mirror Holder!
The One who knows
She is my perfect Reflection.

*

Bismillah!
i make the Heart hajj,
walking through crushed-
stoned soft-sanded Deserts,
whistling to Barren Birds
of all this bleakness.
Their songs are so up-lifting.
i'm fucking floating in their sea songs,
reminding my bones
that i'm walking on their Brothers,
underneath the canopy
of our ancestors.
i pass a Crow with an almond
in her mouth, and the colossal
wreck ramses, Shattered Face too!
But fuck! My heart is beginning
to swell and swim as i carry
the Skulls and Words and Gems.
i am getting closer.
i am finally getting closer to You.

*

Here, let me fill your Water Cup.
Whoops! i've only poems
in my pitcher. How about
some crumbs leftover
from this bread in my bag?
Whoops again! More poems!

The joking tricks of the Mystic.
Don't worry, though.
My poems will feed you for lifetimes.

*

The Sphinx presented Yousof
a riddle, so i walked up
to her and kissed her on
the forehead and rubbed
her under the chin and
behind her neck.
A Purrrr
means "Yes" to all
of the world's Mysteries.

*

i am a Corpse Flower,
sleeping upside down
on the tops of Mountains,
shouting your Name out
and listening to it return
back to me in Valley Echoes.

Have you heard me
singing to you,
when the skies have gone black,

and your eyes have become heavy?

This time i'll drink from the Clouds
and snack on some Stars to survive.

Now i meditate with closed eyes.
i softly whisper your Name.
i am the Wind.
Look how excited your lavish
lotus hair is to see me!
Dancing about in total free love!

*

And i've slept and lived
alone fine before you!
But there's a difference
in the duality of knowing:
the Warmth from the Cold,
the Partial from the Whole.

*

So much to teach you!
So much more
to learn
from
Your Lips.

*

You mad old mistress, you!
You clever little Planter!
i see what you did there.

You buried the mustard seed
under the Eden tree of my Heart,
right there by the ribs!

My oh my, She is growing limbs.
She is stretching like a beautiful
Autumn Goddess inside of me.
And more beautiful Pain!
…i can hear Her singing!

*

Going to take a break
from all the Listening
and the pathetic scribbling
and pulling Stars out
of my pockets like party tricks...

Just to show You
how much
You deserve
all this fucking loving Kindness.

*

Of all god's children,
i am the most condemned.
The Lover. The Poet.
With open eyes, i see the World
in its truer Form, which hides
Itself from most people.
However, it is in this Great Opening,
where all things flood into
my pores and overtake my body.
The largest Illumination among them: Pain.

*

What on earth did you do to Me!?
Today, i am anything but me.
i am everything all at once.
And how can this be?
This Endless Internal Tingling.
It's the Volcano's Mouth again,
blowing wet-lipped kisses to You.
It is the slow moan and vibration
of original Pangea and the continuing
of the Mountain Flowers opening
their petals and spreading wide
like You are for me.

Fire burns when you are close.
But inside It, all you know is oneness.

Open the Door.
There's none to Love you more.

*

Phantom Limb,
where've you gone?
You were never attached to me,
but somehow i miss you profoundly.
The Secret is that our atoms
are entangled in freedom and
have been since the First Fire.
And like a sugar cube dropped in tea,
i am dissolving back into You.

*

Can i be more than just a Disciple
to all of your divine Love?
i will follow you through all Sandstorms and Floods.
i will shield your face with mine,
i will lift you from Raging Waters and give you my Lungs
to Breathe from.
i will be your Medicine and Cure,
if you are ever Poisoned by anything.

But i know you need Nothing from me.
What could a Peasant Heart ever
give to a Galaxy of Compassion?

Love and Devotion!
Another, more Simple Star, i am,
that you can hang in your Sky.

*

Learn the secrets of the Eternal Song
and all its clever ways,
then lure it out of that Soul Cave
into the bright Light of living day.

Here's the Secret: relax your Mind.
All that is Golden will stay!
Call to your Friend: Come out and Play!

*

True Love is Reverence.
i have turned
my entire body
into a Shrine for You.

*

i tore the Sky out like paper.
The colors and lines weren't quite how i wanted them to
be for you.
i remixed the colors and started anew.
But to save the Creation,
i laid the Sun at your feet
and put the Birds in your Hair to Sing.

*

Like a Wounded Animal
i cried out in Weakness and Pain.

Then i saw Your Face.

And my Heart
fell completely
out of the Sky.

*

So much closer.
So much more powerful.
i dream of you most nights.
So intensely.
i am saving You.
You are kissing me.
All is well and right in the world.
No Words. No Songs.
Only Silence is capable
to describe how Beautiful
your Heart is.

*

Poetry? What is that?
These are Conversations
and Conversions with and of myself.
Things i would wish to say
to You, if i were only
so blessed to be close enough
for you to Hear me.

*

i am a Cave Fish.
My eyes know only Darkness.
Yet, Knowing is my Sight.
Love is my only Vision.

i'll never see it Dance.
i'll never hear it Sing.

Yet, i know the Sun is Rising.
Loving. And i, loving it back.

*

i am Sinking
in Quicksand again.
If it were only quicker.
All my Words and Poems
are Stones i am heaving
into a Giant River of your Soul.

Watch it overflow.

*

Drunk Sufi
blathering
poetry.
Stumbling
like a
crumbling stone
through
the City
of Roses,
Talking to Birds.
Blowing kisses to Flowers.
Knowing they
are You.

*

There are well over
four hundred billion
birds living in the world
at the present moment.
How can it be
that my Bird Heart sings
only, only for One?
only, only for You?

*

Pressing down,
pressing down.
And then.
Release.
Like the Flowers
opening.
The Dirt spreading
its God Lips to kiss

the world again, anew.
Release
in the Bird Wings spanning
like my heart
madly
for You!

*

Shukran!
Shukran!
Shukran!
You are
truly
Everywhere.

My Basket is a giant
multifold universe
Laughing Love into everyone.

i threw my heart in your River
a long, long time ago.

*

Are these
Poems
or
are they
Realities?
or Neither.

*

Tragically Beautiful,
You've been.
You are
like a dead bird,
moanfully crooning
inside, and identical to,
my Heart.

*

i sit, reading
my Brother's Words
with the Friend.
And i am trying so hard
not to cry.
There's so much that's
pouring out of my Glass
and feeding the Clouds.
How can i tell You?
There is no Language.
That Collection of Sounds.
There's more hope
in me pointing at your heart
just Laughing and Crying
at the same time.

*

Teacher of discipline.
The disciple of your Love.
i am.

Learner.
Lover.
Gainer

of All Things
through
your soft Silence.
Your wet Lips.
Your Heart reverberates
like chamber music
in my cenotaph soul.
i am
entirely You.

*

i am Brahma
and Brahmin.
How many Heads
must i possess
just to perceive your Beauty?

My lips fall off me
like petals from a Tree.
i am Rebirth and Regrowth.
You are Everything
inside of me.

Angel wings, melting.
Tempest wings, unfurling.
Love. Reborn. Eternal.

Mountains all collapsing
at the sight of your Smile.

*

i Live in the Silence of your Heart.
My mouth blooming with broken Sound.
The Star dangles like bait for my soul.
The body empty. The Love so full.

*

i became enamored with Thunder
the day your Love filled me with Lightning.
The Oceans and Seas were born in my heart, so i began
flooding Everything,
kissing all the Clouds,
skipping through Streams,
laughing on Water,
watching your Garden grow.

How mad is the Mind when the Heart plays the Drum?
How frantic is my love-singing when i feel your Silent
Smile buried in my chest?

i've never been so Drunk without a single Drop.
So pleased without a single Touch.

*

My heart is a blooming Meadow,
stationary but roaming.
Lost and Longing for your Heart.
i see You everywhere.
All these Flowers erupting
inside me are your Touch.

In my thirst, i am transformed.

i become a Love Fox,
licking your wet Eyes,
kissing your Face.

There exists so much
beyond our Names.

*

My Friend, the Tavern Keeper,
keeps pouring me drinks.
In this Sisyphean continuance,
one drains, another is filled.
i reply that i have already
been too full for too long.

"You are an infinite vessel.
Keep drinking with eager lips."

Eager Lips! i shout
and try to get onto my feet.

The Glass shatters. The Friend laughs.

"Look how Drunk you are
off of Love's Wine!"

i Smile and Wail for your Lips.

My Mouth has been closed
and billowing incense without you.
Beautifully aching in Silence.

You reach your hand to take mine.
i feel you moving Inside me.

"Have another sip.
The Ocean will never Overflow.
And neither will you."

*

In all my Wanting,
i tore the Mask off
the Face of the World.
i had grown too weary
in all my wondering.
Too sleepy-eyed from all
the illusions lurking.

Your smile and kiss:
i have seen everywhere.
i have known all along.

*

Am i a blurred Nightmare?
A Wild Horse running
through your Dreams?
i came here to Drink from You.
To wet my Lips with Yours.
How else am i to Sing
with a broken voice?
Today i counted every petal
the Rose held in an embrace.
Let the Joyful Cry!
i have seen your Face.

*

Every utterable Sound
is a Love Letter
from my mouth to Yours.
Every Breath,
Lips kissing your Ground.
i lie Naked under the Tree,
awaiting your Rain.
My Soil is ripe for all your Seeds.

*

Let me be
the only Cup you own.
Fill me.
Let my hand
become Yours.
i love you so much.
Raise me into Light.
Blow your Breath through me
and i'll make Music.
All i ever want
is to Dissolve into you entirely
and for your lips to be mine,
so i can Kiss the whole World.

*

How many Fires
have you started in me?
Am i that easy?
Built to burn
inside and outside
and only for You.

How many Deserts
have you transformed
into Meadows?

How many Gardens and Seas
from Empty Space
inside my Chest?

How many Earthquakes
have you prevented?
How many lives saved?
How much Love
have you Given?

This, and many other Things,
i wish to Know.

*

i am your Naked Mouthpiece,
and it's funny when you
Talk like this.
So filled with Reckless Abandon.
The only Power is Love.
And your playful and gentle Touch
Breaks and Heals me.

i am skinned alive,
Laughing at all
the Stars you hid in me.

*

Babcia,

Have you led me to this
Beautiful Land
to finally Grow like a
Happiness Flower?

i managed not to Cry
on your Birthday.
Because i know they are your Tears.

i am sorry that i've ignored your
Laughing in the Trees, telling me.
i am here Now. *Wounded*, yet here.

i see You every time i'm Smiling.
You were the Vortex of Butterflies
Singing inside my Lungs.
You were the fresh-bloomed Roses
tickling my Sleepy Eyes.

Love was not just what you showed
me. It was what you showed
me how to Give.

Multivalent, i've lain on the Ground.

To Become. To Be. To Become.

DYING

*

Listen to the earth.
Follow your intuition.
And dissolve
into a raincloud.

*

Remember:

Forgiveness
is bigger
than Us.

*

And i will Laugh
with the Innocence
of a Child
on the day
Death shows His face.
Because i am Him
and He is me.
An extension of me,
like a Brother.

My Light will pour out
and over the glass,
toppling. i will laugh
knowing,
Truth exists...
even with her tattered
& gilded Wings.

*

But i gave up
thinking a long
time ago.

What is the
need for thoughts
once you know
that anything
you can ever think
comes from the Great
Lungs
of Everything
in a Single
Breath?

We are Stars,
like a burning
sun Rising.

So Know, deeply,
that the Eye
which perceives
is made
from the Materials
of Everything.

Then, It simply
see's *All*,
all of the time.
Because It is,
as i Am
and You Are!

Like leaf-covered
Lovers under
the Moon,

We all will Be.

*

Why else do we
Weep when our
Beloveds die?

To Water
the Soil
for them to
Grow Again.

*

But alas:
She was a Woodpecker.
And i,
the Cedar Tree.

Pecked
full of Holes,
i watch her Wings
fly far from me…

*

Somewhere
in the Soft
Morning Sky,

i blended
with the Sunlight
so i'll never die.

*

i know
nothing
of You,

except those
Rosebushes
swaying in
the Wind
within your Eyes.

There are
so few
briars,
my eyes
can perceive.

So.

Please,
Teach me
more
of You.

*

Word of the Day: Orogenesis

So Remember, that even
our Greatest Mother
trembles and quakes
in her knees
right before new
Mountain Ranges
spring to Life
from Her Deepest Heart.

*

Jeez, man.
More posthumous
releases.

i've been *dead* for Years.

*

Why be so intimidated
by so much Beauty?

Let the Pain flood your atoms.
Let it eat you Alive.

*

Let me
die
Weeping
inside
the
Door
of
Your
Soul.

*

i must've left a Window open.
i hear you down there,
in my Heart's Basement.

It sounds like so many
things are Breaking...

Beautifully.

*

i'm sorry.
i got wrapped up in all my plans.

i forgot i am only a part of Yours.

*

Oh, i'm sorry...
Are you not God?
Are you not the Mirror
of All that i See?
Of Everything that
We could ever Speak?

*

Sparticle:

Dance with me upon
a carpet of Stardust in the Desert
to this Quantum Entanglement Tune.
My Heart is Yours.

Yes, my dear, your Eyes
are the most beautiful i've ever seen.
But take my hand.
Show me your Supersymmetry.
Let my Light
Live
in your Dark Matter.

*

Psyche,

Brother Zephyr blows
your kisses to me.
And i lay Garlands
at your sleepy bedside.

i pray to my Star Kin
to Awaken Dreams.

i'd gladly give up my Wings
for you to empurple my Night.

-Cupid

*

In Nakedness, i came.
And in it i shall go.
But in between
passing through
the Wilderness,
where i trace your
eyes in the dark
amongst the Leaves,
waiting for the Stars
to drop their Spears:
i Long, longer than
most will ever know.

*

When my heart becomes
a dark and empty
Winter Home,
i light the Candle
and sit by the Door
to await patiently
your Return to me
like springtime leaves
to the sycamore tree.

*

Abscission:

You fell from me
like browned leaves
and the ripe fruit.

A Moulting of the Soul.
An Enlightening of our former selves.

Metamorphed, We are now
Butterflies, and our wings fill the sky,
as i Klimt kiss your Gold-flaked Body.

Underneath the Moonlight,
the Mushrooms blow in our Breeze.

*

Al-Inshirāḥ:

i find Sleepy Solace in your Soul,
where i can Rest my head.

i find Comfortable Comfort in your Eyes,
where i can Rest my lips.

Allah Allah Allah

*

Dear God,
You Know i never
ask for much,

and you've given
me the Wisdom
to know better
than to ask for Anything.
But my Heart Yearns so much.

i only ask for One Bird out of Your entire Sky.
Only One Star out of Your Magnificent Universe.
Only One Grain of Sand from the Whole Majesty of
every Desert and Beach.

i only need One.
One Drop of Rain.
To fill
My Lonesome Bucket.

*

i've died ten thousand
deaths just today.
And in every time
the Wind blows,
i am entirely reborn.

i have Jewels to Give to your Mind.

Right within your grasp,
i am a Pillar of Light.

*

Your Eyes were the most
Benevolent and Comforting
Universe i ever had the
privilege to Live inside.

And i've found Them again
in a Distant Sky
that You led me to
with all your Love.

i, now knowing, that you've
still been Here,
Loving me all along.

*

If you possessed
the Golden Lamp
to grant me
only one wish,
it would be this:

Let me, let me,
please let me
Care
for
You.

*

Quick!
Pluck
the Leaf.

Or It'll
Pluck
you back.

*

After Childish Ego,
the Intellect Illusion prevailed.
But then you cut my Sight
sharper than heaven knives.
Now all i can See
is what You see through my Eyes.

Everything is Love.
Everything is Alive.
Everything is Humming Divine.

*

"And Jacob kissed Rachel,
and lifted up his Voice,
and Wept."

Where are the Stars,
that underneath,
i once Slept?

Curl your back like Waves
kissing my Shorelines,
over all Horizons,
like the incoming ship.

*

Cut off my Head,
and my Blood
will pour into the soil,
for All Things to Grow again.

*

We are all One and the Same.
We Rise from different Climes
and different Soils
that produce different Results
in this Natural World.

So perform an ego-ectomy
on yourself.
i promise it's all for the best.

When was the last time you
saw a group of Daffodils
passing judgement?

*

Cut out my heart.
Blend it to liquid.
Walked across the World
and Poured it in your River.

This is the End of Me.

*

Detach yourself!
Unbridle your Wings!
from this cultural
illusion and this
society of bullshit!

Hide yourself in the Woods.
Kiss all the Trees
and Make Love with Nature.

It's your only hope.

Sew your Universe
back into the Patchwork
of the Night. Bind yourself
to the universal in Everything.

*

Why swim against
all currents with a sad soul!
Even the Fish will wear
itself out quickly that way.
Your body was not born
to Breathe in the Waters.
So let it go.
Drift along
in Love's Lightness
like a free'd leaf
along the Water's Caress.

What Unbearable Lightness!
What Torturous Beauty!

*

i've walked on too many
Solipsistic Sylvan Paths
lined with the Tears of Trees,
and i myself have lain down
so many times just to Kiss
the ground that touches your feet.

And my own wet eyes
have poured into the earth,

My Heaven,
My Home.
My Dear,
i am so Alone.

Can we Dance to one last Song,
before i walk this world forever long?

*

i am so easily
lost in the ruins
of my mind,
and when i begin
to wonder what i should do...
i remind myself,
it's so simple.

There is only one thing
we can ever do:

Surrender.
Surrender to it All.

*

And how so easily
us Lovers are the
Snake Skin. We
transform someone
with our Love,
and then they Moult us.
i am an Empty Husk
left behind on the Grass.
Forgotten.

*

My fallaciously infallible
Thoughts and Words.
Oh lord, for how long
have i Searched my life
for the Great Unfindable?
Only You Know my truths.
Because they are Yours.
Line my path with just a few
more of your Precious Gems
and Crystals and Bones,
and i'll make my way back
to Her Holy Land, Her Paradise!
It's coming soon, i can tell.
My Bones will rest upon
the jagged mountain peaks
beneath the Sky's Roof,
where my flesh will become
its True Form: Nothingness.

i am Food for Vultures.

*

Thankfully, there is always
Rebirth in Immolation,
because in my Childish
Moth Life i've followed the Light
of your Stars, looking to find You.
But again and again and again,
almost seemingly never-ending,
i flew into the Buddha's Candlelight.
Illumination and Happiness
and Compassion and Destruction.

But Death and Rebirth are always more holy
the subsequent time around.
And now i know the tricks
the eyes play and will not
be deceived again and again.
Well, i might. i am a Fool
above all other things.

But i see your shimmering Stars,
and i flap my Eternal Wings
toward only You,
with Nothing
but Kisses
on my Lips.

*

"Why do you love?
Or even more: how do
you love me?" She asked.

My ego pondered
without speaking:
Why? How?
How could i not?
You are Everything that
makes my soul complete
and feel the Cold Breeze
that carries all Birdsong
and Beauty within
and without me.
You Fill me, my Being,
with Comfort and Happiness
beyond all realms i've ever
known or could ever touch.

But instead of saying
those simple things,
i said: 'See'
as i held
the Ruby into the Sunlight.
Without saying anything
for a little while, allowing
Her Mind to simply
Watch this Act occur.

Then i leaned in close
to her cheekbones and
looked deeply into Her
eyes. Now i spoke to Only
and All of Her:

Like the Sunlight Inside
the Ruby making it Glow,
Your Love has slept inside
me since before All Creation.
i have always and will
always love you like This.
It is when You are Near,
like the Sun, that i
become Entirely Illumined.
We are the Same.

*

i am a Little Bee.
Wings coated in Honey,
drowning on the water's surface
of your Heart's Wishing Well.

i came here with Love
thick on my Lips
to wish you well.

Maybe you'll hear
my soft singing inside You
and lift me up
in Your Beautiful Hands.

*

You're an Abandoned House,
and i've been knocking on
Your Door for decades now.

يوسف the Creator of Impossibilities.
The Opener of Angel Wings.
The Searcher of The Unfindable.
The Recoverer of The Irreplaceable.
The Prophet of Love's Lips.

i will keep knocking softly,
because i swear i hear the floor
boards creaking, and they have been.
i hear your Sweet Voice Singing,
somewhere hidden away
in the Attic, blowing all the Dust
of my Mind around for Lifetimes.

*

My God,
why do i wail
or talk at all?

Why this instinctual
lowering of my Bucket
into the Familiar Well?

All i, i mean You, say
has all been said before.
Shall we Dance to this
broken record some more?

But only the fool believes in choice.
i see the Painting in all its Grandeur.
Let's play that one again,
so i can Sing across Time to her sleepy head!
You are the Design and the Needle
dropped into my Wax and Grooves.
All my songs are songs to You!

*

Samsāra:

…Eat Alone
Drink Alone
Sleep Alone
Die Alone…

*

Bismillah,

Please. Please.
Do not be another Prophet Test.
Be not the Languid Grapes
hanging before the Red Fox's Mouth.
Prithee, be the Only Divine

Gift that i'll ever need,
that i never deserve beyond
Your Immaculate Grace.

i am Selfish and Sad, i'll admit,
in my Longing and Weakness.

But i see Her, entirely
as my only other face.

You are the Clay Maker, my dear.
And i've lain in this Kiln for ages.
Only you can make two into one.
To make the only Truth of Oneness,
which is never the combining,
but instead the revealing
of the always eternal connection.

Please let her be my only one,
that one i am meant to be
baked into to make the Whole.

*

i am at your Footstool.
A Beggar. Love's Peasant.
Look how ragged and weary
my Heart is and has been.
i only have Sad Offerings for You.
And they are all myself.
i deserve nothing.
But. But if in Your Grace
and Compassion, you could
open The Gates, where Your
Eden Fruits were once always Ripe.

There is only one of your Grapes
that i ever wish to Taste.
Only one Flower Petal from your
entire Garden of Majesty,
One grain of sand from your Deserts,
to keep me company.
A Companion and Guide for Hearts,
to walk hand in hand,
back to You.

*

i have been walking through
the darkest forest my entire life,
and a Light led me towards the edge,
where i saw You from the outline
of the branches looming upwards.
You were sitting by the River laughing,
so i came and sat by You,
and joined you Completely.

*

Please show me the way.
i myself have given up in the trying.
A World that begs for the Future
but is tired of the Cruelty of Chess
and the Loveless.
How many more white flags
must i stab into my dying bones?
Only one thing left to do.
Only one remaining thought:
only the Here and Now.

Someday, i'll die in it.

*

i am ready for death.
i await her cold kiss
on all my dark nights.
Slip into the soft shadows
of my sleepless room.
Burn my hand-woven life tome.
Let us walk away now,
slow and beautiful,
like Gold becoming Air.

*

The Giving is better than any money.
If i ever stop writing this Poetry for You,
then please place me in your Grave.
And i'll become the Sun and the Shade.

*

Concurrent Hearts.
Circumnavigation.
We are drops of rain.
So many to fill an Ocean.
We *are* the ocean.
All the Light Years
of atoms your body contains.
i also contain yours in mine.
Sphere-Shatterer.
Does the mountain point
upwards or inwards?
When i want to stretch
my Love into the Sky,
i kneel and kiss the ground.

i am Dying before i die. A Mystic.

Everything i ever touch
will Melt
from all my Longing.

*

i don't have
to look for You.
You are inside me.

i don't have
to want to hear your Laugh.
It's my atoms vibrating.

i don't have
to kiss you ever.
It's the volcanic swarm
of Butterflies
tickling the insides
of my ribs.

*

Welcome.
To the Tangible
of the Most
Intangible
in All Existence
of All Universes!

*

Drunk.
Whistling.
Marching towards
the Gallows
of this Love.

*

The laughing smoke.
The trembling sky.
Quickly you came.
Quicker you go.
Die before you die.
Let everything go.

*

"You're going to die
very soon," They said.
"Good. Thankfully."
i Replied.
i've been Waiting
and Longing
My Whole Life.

Time for the Flower
to Open into Light.

*

i am your Oyster.
Your holy Clam Shell.
Pluck my Pearl.
Put me in your Mouth.
Spit it out.

Crush it to Powder.
Brush it into your Skin.
i am Nothing.
i am Everything in You.
i am.

*

Friend, my soul
is the Grain.
Crush it more
and make
your Bread.
i'll Die a thousand Deaths.
i'll Feed millions.
Do you know how much i love?
Ha! That's a silly question.
i *am* Love. i am the Wind and Rain.
Everyone knows my kiss
in some way or form,
which is Yours.

*

So they piled the bodies high
and sang "that which lives shall never die!"

*

i love seeing lovers in Love.
Because Love is
the only emotion i now know.
i've shed so many Skins.
They've all made me Grow.
i've kissed Sand Dunes

and Deserts and Palms
and swallowed Dates Seeds
and Hallucinogenic Angels.
i've Danced in Mountains
and stood upside down.
So many times i've Laughed
at Disaster and Licked
her sad Face. Do you know
how many times i've thought
of you and Dreamt of you?
i have been your unburdened life.
i have been your Soul,
crying from Darkness
and Longing for Light.

*

How many times have i
come here to Die?
How many times have i
set myself on Fire
at your Doorstep
too afraid to ring your Bell?
i used to think too much.
Now i don't think at all.
i just Die.
Everywhere i go.

Love has no expectations or wants.
No demands or desires.

There are Flowers curling
out of your Lungs
breaking their Necks
to blow me Kisses.

And i am the Sun,
the Only Star that is Burning
myself selflessly for your Love.

Don't hurt yourself.
Smile More.
Burst into Bloom.
And bend your Body toward me
and Eat me up.

*

Remember, friends.
That which we see as Traumatic
to our selves and egos
are very faint and trivial
to the Whole, so be not
wearied by Anything.

i assure you:
the Stars do not give a fuck.

So relax and take it easy.
Continue to love.
Because if that's all you have,
it's the only thing worth having.
The Earth cannot exist without the Sun,
but the Sun can without the Earth.
Learn to see the difference.
Let your *self* dissolve into this Light.

*

Drunken Midnight Sky, burn.
My bones are firewood.
For You. For Her. For Me.

Collapse like my heart
under all this Dukkha.
Breathe Life into my broken lungs.
Give us True Moksha.
The Freedom of the Blushing Flower,
who knows your Secret Silent Word.

i've dissembled my soul
like a wooden bird
at both of your feet.
So why does my heart
still catch on fire
and i disintegrate
into the Wind
simply when she walks
away Laughing,
with You sitting like Buddha
in her tangled eyes,
Calling Calling Calling,
without language?

The only love i know
is the love of defeat.

*

Everyone i know and love
is Dying tonight.

The soft song is languid
in a beautiful timbre

that reverberates
and resonates
the eternal OM,
panging in your heart,
breaking down the Doors.

*

What doesn't kill you
makes you stronger.
What does kill you
breathes new life into you.

Kill yourself or be Killed
by all the Blooming Light
that is billowing out of your Chest.

Keep your mouth shut
& your mind quiet.

Laugh at yourself
and Die.

i look at you & start smiling.

i Recognize
that i have loved only You
my entire life.

*

Coup-de-grâce:
Your Love-blow to my heart
has left me Dizzy,
wandering the streets

silently calling your Name
and peering deeply
into Beautiful Faces in search of You.

All Suffering is Necessary
to truly know your Joy.
Every drop of Pain:
Nourishment for Soul Soil.

Thigmotropic, i grow and encircle
Your Invisible Hands
just like Plants reach Upwards
Grasping at Light.

*

Is your Heart
a Honeysuckle Vine?
Are your legs
Heavy with Rapture?

Eternal Sleep is afoot.

*

Our first date:
We tore off our Clothes
and ran Naked through the Woods,
until we came to a Stream.
You kissed me there.
And we jumped in together
and Dissolved.
To this day, we've never left.
We are still there.

LIGHT

*

This is the absence of pain,
where I can't stop growing
towards the Light.

*

Open yourself.
Be an exploding star.
Come out of your shell.
Become the seed.
Lie in the dirt.
Eat the Light.

*

Only by continuous grinding
of the holy grain
between
my
Teeth,
do i have any hopes
of my lungs Flooding with Moonlight.

Inside my Mouth,
Slumber All Eternal Songs.

*

And i, the Confused Atheist,
will one day lay in your arms
and weep, my lord. Oh,
because deep down i've always
known, but like a Sullen Child
left alone to only my Room,
the Empty Room of my
own soul, i only did Long more
than others for your Love and
your all-encompassing Light of
Pure Compassion.
Yes, i've known all along your Being.
i've only hoped for a Kiss,
which i knew would come,
which i knew would emit so
much Light of all spectrum shades.
You are the Rainbow, curling out
of my mouth, day and day again,
as living words upon every page.

*

Fuck,
the human spirit
really is plagued
with Loneliness.

Every last one
of us poor bastards.

But Lighten up
just a little bit,
literally like a feather.

Because you can
float into my
Heart anytime
You'd like.

i Promise i only Give.
i never take.

*

What on earth
has happened to me?

i've been losing
more Weight
than of my Mind
recently, and that's
just Madness to me.

Maybe it has
something to do

with fasting
for a quarter
century in my Cave.

i suppose
i'll go out today
and Eat a few
Spoonfuls of Light.

*

The Wordless
Love of Light
and Unspokeness,
like the Seed
that only Whispers
its true self
into the Soil
in Silence.

We Feel,
as it is,
All we need
if we Listen
without Ears.

*

To call you a Dream
would be a grave insult.

Dreams a mere inventions of
the human mind.
A wonderful, yet small thing.

Beyond it are Realms
and Dimensions far outside
all and any of our Understanding.

This is the World you have
Come to me from.

*

So many that i
have Given my
heart to in an
act of Compassion
have taken it and chewed it up.

But while they're picking
it out of their teeth,
and licking their claws clean,
and trying to digest it,
it's going to change them.

And besides, no real loss
was ever received by me.

i grow a new heart continuously
like Flowers
in the Dark
where All the Meadowlarks Sing.

*

Phototropic Brevity.
Awakening. Blooming.
Clouds dispersed
to let in Love and Light,

my petals stretched
like lips to You.

Now where is the Sun?
My sad heart
lingers and longs.

But mind knows,
Light is Eternal
and Always Present
even in Nighttime Darkly Blues.

*

The Trees hold ancient
Knowledge and possess
the most meditative Souls.

Yes, quiet now. We don't
want god to know
i'm sharing more of Her Gold.

Look to archetypes and mythology,
i swear.
How could a sad silly soul like Siddhartha
become the Buddha?

He sat at the foot of the Pipal Tree,
until it breathed Whispered Secrets
into his beautifully receptive Soul.

You are an Empty Cup.
We all are.
Know this,
so they fill you up.

*

Like a delicate child
with an angel's soul,
you've been throwing
snowballs in my heart.
And i'm rolling around
in all the snow, just
trying to keep it
from melting away.

*

And though my heart
may give way like
Mountains into the Sea,
i'll walk this Desert
in shadows of darkness,
still writing your Name
like poetry in the sand.
And i'll Kiss every Firefly
and Bird within my reach
in hopes they'll land
beside you someday
to uplift your Heart,
if it should ever become
too heavy for you, Love.

*

Reach out!
Kiss the World!
She'll kiss you back
and fill your Abyss
with Overwhelming Light.

*

Act on
what you've
always wanted,
what you've
always Loved.

And you
will be Cradled
with Light
like a
Forest Fire
in my Heart.

*

A Fugitive from
the Multiverse.

i've got the Keys!
i've got the Keys!

To Unlock
Everything
you will
ever need.

*

Amrita-lipped Goddess,
Your Mouth
is the only Fruit
i ever
want to Taste.

Soma-souled Lover,
Your Body
is the only Paradise Gate
i ever
want to Open.

*

Heavenbird,
come out and play.
You are welcome to stay.

i am your Sapphire in the Mud.
i may get you a little Dirty,
but i swear that it's okay,
cause i'll clean you off.

And now you Hold with you
quite the Treasure.

*

You long for me
to touch you,
and the days will
soon linger and come.

Inside, you will be
another Great Flood,
overflowing all
of your gemstone cells
with a Greater Love.

i will wash you clean,
removing all suffering,
and like the Word,
you'll dance on the Prophet's Tongue.

*

i am
the Pillar of Light.
Come close to me
with your Pure Heart,
and i will Fill you with
the Sun and erase all
worry from your mind.
i will give you paradise,
and in my arms you can finally rest.

But approach me
with an impure heart,
i will gently Blow on you
like a Dandelion and scatter
you back into our Mother's Womb.

Even god and i fuck up some
of the Ingredient Ratios,
when we've been out
Drinking too much.

*

You've shown me!
Again, again, again.
In my Infinite Nighttimes,
All Darkness, encapsulating,
darker and darker, darker.

Every cave and catacomb
i've crawled out of,
my claws bloody and shed,
like a seed husk, like the crab.

i've left that old body behind
to roll around, like a Wolf in the Snow,
basking in Brighter Light than before.

*

Hush the madness
behind your eyes...

i am a Supernova.
i'll eat your Pain alive.

*

Stare into the Sunlight more,
if you want to be Illumined,
if you want to be Enlightened.

i'm serious.

it won't burn out your Eyes.
Don't believe everything
people say. Cause i'll tell you:
doing that will burn out your brain.

*

Try new things.
i swear our survival depends on it.
Try whispering to your food
before you eat:
"i love you i love you i love you."

*

Wanderer of Light,
You've arisen from the depths
of my deepest oceans,
like a Pearl forming
through foam
into gorgeous Form,
making Mountains weep
and weak knee'd Buddhas
fall under your Spell.
You are the Breath of heaven
amongst all this hell.

*

Some days the world
just looks ugly.

i close my eyes,
but there are more
horrors there that i hide.

So i stand on my head,
and Everything is Beautiful again.

*

Oh dear god,
how many Stars
are Weeping tonight,
knowing that their
lovers somehow
got to be
so far from
one another?

But what's that?
Their Tears bring Spring?

Then be careful:
i'm Sprouting up between your Boots!

*

What fools to yell:
"There he is! The Pillar of Light!
Quick! Capture him in this
Cloak of Shadows and chain
him to the Blackest Trees!"

Morons to not know that they
chase like cats the laser pointer.

There's a difference between the
Light and the Source of the Light.
The Source *is* the Light.
The light simply is.

In ignorance, they live in darkness,
but the Light is still attainable.
How fucked we'd all be if someone
actually did flip the Switch.

*

String Theory:

And when you cry out
from the pain,
it is just the needle prick
to let you know you are being Woven.

Remember that awakening
is a slow process.
You are more like a sugar cube,
sweetie, dissolving in the Friend's tea.

And time is only as real as
we allow it to be.

Know me as your Waterwheel,
as i will gather what you need
to drink and weep it from me.
So your Grains can become Bread.
So your Seeds can become Meadows.
So your Eyes will become Vineyards.

Never forget communal Oneness.
The Wind's Breath can quickly
turn the Ocean into a billion Waves.
The Sun can shine through a prism
and show you more of its Insides.

i've been here for Billions of Years.
i've Danced in the Riverbed,
singing and smiling, at the foot
of Your Most Precious Garden,
and before there was even

the Garden or the Riverbed!

Ponder this idea: Stones and Trees
and Footpaths in the Woods will
always Teach more than classrooms.

And this: People are Intimate Doors
that are begging to be Opened.

Put your weariness in my Basket.
i am inside the Granary,
and there's Beauty that cannot
be spoken, but i can try to *show* you.

But here in this Giant Heart,
there lives an Elephant in the Dark.
There are no Eyes that can See or
Candles to illumine except trust

in the fact that the Universal Hand
is holding you gently as always.
And into the Nighttime Nebula,
Your Beauty is Being Woven.

*

Always know that hard truths,
as well as difficult decisions,
will lead to Beautiful Outcomes.
Just as Hard Rains lead to the
sustenance of all life and a great
proportion of the Earth's Beauty,
which is continually overlooked
by pain in neglect to this simple Truth.

*

For years, i've been seeking
the Self-Immolation of Freedom,
and then i found You.
And your Light consumed
me from the inside,
so now i'll burn forever.

*

And when you're upset
that someone just broke all your windows,
Remember that the Light
is about to come Pouring In.

*

Mouthless Songbird,
Who Stole your Voice?
Who Hollowed your Bones?
Who Painted your Living Corpse?
Who made me question
the Only Unquestionable?
Who allowed only *me*
to Hear your Pretty Song?

*

Ipseity:

You were Here.
Like a Flower.
Then trampled
by running Children.

You were Here.
Like a Butterfly.
Then i lost
you to the Wind.

You were Here.
Like Footsteps.
Along the shoreline,
then the Waves came.

The more i understand,
the less i will Speak.
The more i become,
the less i will Be.

Circles
and
Phosphene.

i am a Puddle, my Sun.
Continue to drink me.

*

This ladder never ends.
Keep climbing
through the Bristles
and Thorns that steal
your Blood away from
you with Laughing.
Laugh back at them.
Let your tears flood
the Seas and Streams
beneath you, so they

may sing back a beautiful
song for your Climb.

The Climbing never ends.
So do not stop.

High above the birds
and bustle below,
the Love Song only
gets louder
up
Here.

*

Someone
holds my heart
with angel hands.
Someone
dances barefoot
in my mind.
All the Laughing.
All the Crying.
i hear them as the same song.
We play different notes.
We play different instruments.
But this Loving
is Unending.
Never does anything
ever go to seed.
Enter your Garden and Weep,
your hands full to Sow.
You'll return Singing,
Arms Full of Sheaves.

*

i was born
with the Swallowed Key.
Foolishly, i thought
that i'd never be unable
to unlock the Box
it belonged to.
But as time went on
i sharpened my mind
on Stone and Flowers,
and the key began to move.
The Box had been inside me.
And i Laughed
as the key turned
in the key hole,
because it tickled so much,
especially when all the Light
came crawling inwards
Dancing along the hardwood
toward your little feet.

*

Coldness and Loneliness
are just beautiful sensations
that you give me to sleep soundly
in your Warm and Loving Heart.

*

Naked and Drunk,
i am holding a Flashlight,
searching through Needle Stacks
and Desperate Deserts.

Foolishness. i now know i am.
i've been looking for only You.
And you, you sly devil, my Friend.
You've made no Match.
i am the Key.
Yet the Keyhole doesn't Exist.

What else is there to do?
i'll *die*.

And become Light,
cause i have some Silent Words
that need to meet your Lips.

*

i had to go see my doctor today
to ask how many more Roses
could grow in my Mouth
and become your Speech?
How many more Bougainvillea
could grow like Capillaries
throughout and to my Heart?

My Body has become a Garden
for all of your Slobbery Kisses.
And my Third Eye, the Mustard Seed,
Laughing as the Shell comes off.

How much longer could i go on
Blinded with Diamond Eyes?

Why is the Trumpet Note
so Sad and so Long?

If your Love brought me here,
then please take me Home.

i am Climbing like Vines
toward your Light.

My Heart is a Jazz Funeral,
while you just sit there
Smiling at me.

*

i have become so Flammable
to every thing around me.
One Spark of Beauty
and i am a Great Lamp,
walking and windblown.

And You are the Light.
You are All of the Light,
emanating out of me.
Nothing remains hidden.

All has been revealed.

There exists no division
between Light and Flame.

*

Face in hands
weeping.
For years i've seen
mountains grow
out of me.

Why are you too afraid
to climb to this Summit?

Don't fear. A hand awaits you.

It will Lift you Here, to me.

Where the Unnamed
Flowers grow so easily.

POLISHING

*

You are a Mirror
of my soul.

An Echo of all
I've ever Thought.

*

Be Kind to strangers.

What the fuck do either
of you have to lose?

*

For days, for months,
for years…

i hid myself
from the world
and love and
friends, only
to create my
own End.

i reduced myself
to nothing
but a simple
Singularity.

Stretched across
the glorious
night sky,
but so alone.

Necessity.

All reduced
to a singular point
will again burst
into radiant
fire colors and light

and pour life
back into
everything
once
again.

*

It took Hemingway
26 years to write
his first novel;
indeed a doozy.

And Van Gogh 28
before he smeared
the universe onto
the Holy Canvas.

And i, now in
the in-between
of them, have
realized that
i Searched
for a Love
much greater.

Which on earth,
it is only the Mirror,
the Reflection of it,
not the genuine
Source,

which i now
fill my mouth
with, as my
heart burns like
10,000 Suns
100,000 Skies
1,000,000 Galaxies

that all, simply,
lead back
to only You.

*

You Persian dust-rattler!
How many Tombs
and Mountains
and old Rugs
in the Abyss
of my Soul

are you going
to shake out?

Because everyone
is starting to
choke on
all the
Dust.

*

Science, i can
only define as thus:
the modern cult
of mostly atheists,
brains enlarged and
beautiful, but some
egos that follow
that growth also.

Virgo Supercluster?
Yes, i know Her intimately.
i often kiss her cheek
on my way
home every evening.

i can see
infinityfold farther
just when
i close
my eyes.

*

Frantically
in Love,
i am climbing
the Highest
Vine

with a Thousand
Thorns in my
sides.

Dripping,

dripping
Love
down to
the earth
below.

*

Life Tip:

Fall in Love with Strangers.
Around every corner.
In every park.
On every crowded bus ride.
Under lights.

And at farmer's markets.
Dance in the Seas of their Eyes.
Let them Flood with your entire Being.

*

We are winter children.
Born babies into the cold.

So our Hearts learned
to be Warmer.

Out of survival,
we Loved Greater than others.

*

Indeed, a Conscious
cleansed like
the Doors of Perception.

Don't ever let there be
any Misconception.

*

Trichiliocosm:

Love and I
are Dancing
on a carpet in the Sky
with Billions
of Marbles underneath it,
with billions of tiny people
with all their tiny lives.

Open and Expand your Mind.

She calls to You,
to take my hand
to Dance with me,
cause she's overwhelmed
at the Energy swelling inside,
while i've been gazing at You.

*

Trying to shed my mind
of the illusion of possession.
We own nothing, and when
we allow ourselves to think
that we do, we ourselves are owned.

There are Freedoms and Prisons
in love like in anything,
but you can choose.

Either way,
it is a difficult Path traveled,
where my Tears line
the dirt roads to make Flowers grow
and to cover my tracks,
to only give, to give the
simplest offering to You.

*

i only ever want to use
my Holy Mouth to kiss Her.

But in truth, i am a Fire-Breather.
With one sneeze alone,
i can reduce all your
Forests to Piles of Ash.

So why are you so hellbent
on tickling the Divine's Nose?

*

Hang a leg out from
your covers tonight.
Feel the Cold, so you
may more deeply know Warmth.

Hang your Empty Basket
out of your window tonight,
so my Rain may overflow it.

Focus on your
Loneliness tonight,
so you may know the Truth,
when i come and fill you up.

*

In times of trouble, remember this:
Cast no Shadows into your Heart.
For it can be a dark place by itself.

Be like the Birds:
Two Wings that must
work together in Balance
and in Harmony.

Otherwise: We, like them,
spiral ourselves
wildly out of control.

Instead, let yourself
Fly Beautiful and Free.

Let Love Lift you into the Sky.

*

Alas, the Bluejay has returned!
Its tattered Robe shaken
clean from Winter's Blanket.
And i, sitting patiently under
Her have waited, knowing.
When was the last time
i have eaten a single spoonful?
There's no need, cause my
stomach and heart are too full!
The Wisdom of the Roots
buried under soil is
my only bench. Cloaked
in wool, i Kiss the Wind,
Her lovely Breath
graces me in every pure moment.
i'll perpetually pour the
Unemptiable Cup into
my empty body in alms,
letting your rivers cleanse
all of my wounds of lifetimes.

*

Have the clouds
parted their lips
to kiss your beautiful
and shimmery face yet,
Beautiful Songbird that dances
upon the capillary
boughs in my heart?
You play my aorta
like a Flute!
Your songs incinerate
my every atom and then
re-bloom me like oleander.

Nothing can stop this Love
from shining out of me
like lighthouse beacons
to your lost ship at sea.

*

Remember Sadness like this:
It's a fucking ocean wave,
so if you're prepared for it,
it wont even phase you
and you can stand in it
and let it wash over you entirely.
But if you're not prepared,
you're fucked.

*

Try to keep your Perspective:
the mind lingers and longs
for Ideas of Things,
not so much the things themselves.

Meaning this:

We create expectations
and meanings from things.
This includes people or love
or whatever. So
we long for our egocentric
creation more than the thing itself.

This is if you are Deep Thinkers.

If you're not so much so,
you long for merely the Image.
No deeper meaning.

But the Enlightened Thinker?

i believe this is the Root
of Compassion. Giving Love
regardless of expectation
or circumstance, no object.
Merely sharing all that is good inside
of you and projecting it
out into the Universe
for the Benefit of the Other
rather than for the *self*.

In this Soil,
Selflessness is Root.
In the other soil,
selfishness.

*

And if i am meant
to have my own
Personal Angel,
She will come to me
like Leaves to the Tree.
So easily, her wings
will give me Shelter
from all the storms
of this fleeting world.
i hope for it with
all of my pathetic
and lonely soul!
But who i am to know?
You've proven me wrong
so many times when
i beat my fists on your
Gates, screaming your
Most Profane Names!
Then my senses
reemerged and those
childish sensations subsided.
i've laid down on the path,
waiting simply for the Rain.
i know you'll Dust away
all of this Ragged Human Pain.

*

The American Dream:
emptiness

The American Slogan:
that's not my responsibility

*

A delicate angel's destruction
is enough to make you want
to trample all the grains,
but there are one hundred billion
mustard seeds dancing in my veins.
And they're calling your sugar name.
My heart is sleeping and beating
at the center of the world that
you so sweetly walk upon,
vibrating loving calmness into
your mind and heart's vessel.

Little wave, i am your shore.
i've been waiting patiently for you.

*

Love Letters:

Envelopes filled
with Blood.

Pages
typed with Ivory Keys
and Marrow Ink.

Love is giving,
not taking.

No Return
Address.

*

"What are those wavering
lines on the Water's Face?"
thought the Ivory Ibis.
My god! They are Desolation!
They hide my Unattainable
Lover's Face, and this Water
separates us from being together.
But the Water is God's Mirror,
and her sweet Body is rising
more and more toward this Light!
Soon her Face will be free,
and she can rest on her Lily Pad.
i shall feed her the sweetest Fruit,
and she'll never be thirsty
thanks to her Buried Root.

But for now, i must continue to wait,
shrouded in Temporary Pain.

i lay my limbs in the sand
and watch the sun beams
cut through the water
and illumine all of my Love.

*

Remember that sadness leads
to growth and reward. Out of
such sadness and suffering
from being away from the
Great Love of this Universe,
the Birds grew wings to try
and get closer to the Universal
Heart in it all. Now they soar
the blue-eyed skies and absorb

all of the sun's beautiful rays.
Do not run from the sadness.
You cannot run from yourself.
Be at one with it.
Let it change you.

Let it form like Love Mountains
from the Deepest Seas of Yourself.

*

How could i ever lose anything,
when All is contained within me?

How could i ever want anything,
when i already possess Everything?

*

You must know the rain,
to know the drought.
i am the doubter
and the doubt.

*

How does one kiss the Bird
that flies so high and far?
Simple.
You are the Bird.
Kiss yourself, silly.

*

i am.
equally empty.
equally full.
equally wise.
equally fool.
equal song.
equal heart.
equal you.
equal light.
equal dark.

*

Rolled the stone from my sepulchre
to lay in dogwood petals on a side street.
Sang with meadowlarks.
Laughed with crows.
Wrote prose for you.
i could find no cons.

This Longing
is but another song.
A place where
the stars fade into the sun.

This Love
is but a few more blood words.
The place where
lovers do not meet
but are inside each other all along.

This Universe
is precise like a watch tick.
The place where
your breath and the wind are one.

How many birds have died
only wanting
a more beautiful song
to sing to You?

i am just another one of them.

i am lost. You are found.

Love's mouth only knows one word:
Silence.

*

Piano bones.
Play me like a ghost.
Wherever i look
Everyone i see
is You.
Especially
when i look
in the Mirror.

*

Expect nothing.
Only pain.
Pain is the
only guarantee.

Every pain
you give me,
i only see
its true form:
Love

*

Silence.
"Khamush,"
Rumi said.
i love you.
you are
the best
part of me
i have been
looking for
inside of me
for years
but found
inside of You.

*

Who have i really been looking for?
So hard to tell with a cracked and dirty Mirror.
It reflects only partial images.
It points in the wrong direction.
But i've been Polishing the Mirror,
laughing at my surprise
finding
i've been looking for myself
all of this time.
i've been looking for you.
But you've been
dancing inside me
quietly,
saying nothing.
Just smiling. Silent.

*

Curled backbone
like a broken angel,
undeserving of nothing.
My bird mouth is full.
Longing. Song.
Crushed flowers
growing under your feet again.
The moon is a poem
and a kiss on your hand.
But i am entirely fire and flame.
i am not me. i have no name.
Words fall like grapes from a vine.
Give me your mouth.
We are drunk off nonexistence, nontime.

*

Everything you run from
is everything you run to.
And everything you run to
is everything you run from.

The universe throws
banana peels on your course.

And Love spreads her legs.

This is how all
beautiful disaster
ensues.

*

All, ah.
Have i been neglecting
the garden?
Have i been pissing
on the plants?
This soul work isn't easy.
The pickaxe heavy.
My blood tastes cheap without You.
There can only be one sentence.
Three words. *Your* Love.

We've been staying up late.
Laughing in this room alone.
i've grown weary
of everything around me.
Make me blind to this life.
Close all eyes but the third, yours.

Drown me in the River of Light.

*

Synesthete Friend,
i think of your love
and i begin to *taste* beauty.
Your silent eyes
open doorways
within me that go deeper.
All my atoms vibrate.
i look into the Mirror
and all i see is You.
You've told me
this story before.
Laughing,
You threw Lilacs in the Pond.

*

"Those who know don't talk,
and those who talk don't know."
With deep understanding
and awareness, all sense
and desire to speak ceases.
A new form emerges,
arising like a flower's
silent beautiful glory.
In this phase of Grace,
close your mouth,
and you will hear the Voice
of god everywhere.

*

Some days, your little candle
light just wants to come home.
Give me all the suffering
disease and death.
Because i am here to Love you,
until none of me is left.

*

i am searching the dark sea
for your hidden key
to place in the lock and turn.
Break my mind from this crab shell.
Set me free.
i'll eat nothing but light.
And if i must wait,
i'll wait till the next life.
Just to be Near You.

STORIES

*

We are the only ones
stupid enough to wonder why.

Live in the majesty
and madness of all this Love.

*

It is the vultures
who do god's loving work.

*

"There is no god.
If there were,
why would human
beings' natural reaction
to death to be a loss,
to cause suffering,
rather than a joyous
celebration of that person's
soul entering into god's kingdom?"

"Ah, quite," i replied
to the atheist in my mind.
"Perhaps, this perspective
is misguided or misdirected.
It's quite possible that
She (yes, *She*) is not the
controller of our emotional
state, or even more so,
not the one to reign over
our actions. Indeed, that
responsibility and power
belongs to me, within me.

She does not tell men
to murder one another.
She does not invite men
to react with hatred or revenge.
She does not call to
the hearts of men to drive
them to madness and greed.

Early on,
before the stars made the
sun rise,
She planted a seed

deep in the fabric of
your soul; it's that soft
whisper that you hear
like a flute in your
marrow and cells;
ah, but alas,
you *choose* to weep!
you *choose* to kill!
you *choose* to suffer!

Instead, dear friend,
listen closely to that grain.
Water *that* seed
and let it grow.

Existence exists in those
blooming Lilacs underneath
your rib cage...

i'll admit:
it's very faint.
But i promise:
it's always singing your name."

*

Ah, what self-conscious
web weavers we've become.
Out of necessity.
Out of self-defense.

To protect ourselves,
we acrobatically dangle
upside down,
weaving day and night,

so nothing will
ever come that close.

How completely silly we are...

At this point,
who is tangled
in who's web?

*

Can i share a
secret with you?

Well, it goes like this:

The Stars are forever
in our favor;
they burn and burn
to enlighten our way
through all darkness.

They whistle in the night.
And hidden in the day,
they are silently
rooting
for Us.

*

God made me
a special gift
to the world.

But in my naïvety,
i jumped too soon
from Her palm.

And like a baby bird
fallen from Her womb,
my Wings left the nest
and broke in the tree branches...

This, you
(yes, all of you!)
are too.

All i am is the Pond,
reflecting your Beautiful Face back to show you.

*

My strongest instinct
is maternal.
Like a calm mother,
i bent over your wounds
to remove the Splinter
from your skin.
i wiped the Blood away
and Kissed your soft
delicate head.
...then i cried, out of your sight,
behind the Rosebush,
because i know there are
just some that i can't get to.

*

Anyways...

Relax a bit.
Take a load off.

Our Bodies
are just Water,
Dancing to
the Vibration
of the Ocean.

*

You can never make the Flower Bloom.

You can only Water it
and patiently wait.

Besides,
the Magic resides
in its own Essence.

*

Hmph.
Another Solipsistic Song
for my mind to indulge upon:

If there is only the I
yet the i is an *illusion*,
then i can see through
Ten Billion Eyes,
wanting only one pair
to sing back into
from a continuum,

kiln-cooked in
the Cosmo of
those Constellated Moons
that turn the world
upside
down.

*

i am afraid,
terribly afraid...

because i know that great love
always end in great loss.

i don't...no, i cannot
bear the thought
even now,
in knowing.

But i'll be strong.
i'll stay at your side,
until all the Birds in the Sky
stop singing.

If they could even begin
to entertain such a silly idea.

*

Yes, i've read
Neruda, and they
really are lovely
poems.

And Petrarch's sonnets
to his beloved
Laura de Noves.

Beautiful,
yet human infatuation.

The Love i breathe
is from other Dimensions,
distant worlds and heavens.

Perhaps, i challenged
the Creator to a
playful competition.

Only 20 poems to sing of Love?

There's more in the Despair.

Whereas, i have become the Air,
and all the forest trees are pens
and all the oceans are my ink,
and i'll write you a love poem
for every atom in heaven and on earth.

Remember:

Love is an art,
and like any great art,
it will change you.

*

Monogenes:

The missing link
of history's tale,
the Eden fruit
moist in my mouth,

You are.

An undiscovered
flower,
blooming beautifully
and forever growing
like the song
of the whale.

*

If all you know
right now
is darkness,
then i'll tell you this:

Burn your own
fucking bright light'd
path through the night.

*

Ah, yes,
i forgot that all science
and truth is derived from
only a single, subjective
observation! Must be why
i lost my mind in seeking

truth, looking to try to see
to the bottom of the ocean.

When *your* truth is but
a shallow stream!

Thank god it takes less
than 2 inches
to drown yourself
in your ignorance!

*

Psssst! Here's a secret:
Don't think, *feel*.

But learn how to think
and think and fucking
think until you want to
blow your fucking brains out.

Then you'll always know
what the beautiful thing to do is,
and you won't even have to think about it.

You'll be free to just love
beyond bounds.

*

How can people live
with such cruelty
in their hearts?

Don't let the sadness
and loneliness eat
away and hollow
out your chest.

Truth is, we all feel this,
and it's what binds,
not separates us all.

*

There are very few times
you will always be in the right,
maybe only one.

It's Love.
Loving is never wrong.

*

Dhyāna

Life and awareness are like this:

We sit silently
in the hollow
tombed museum,
staring at Monet's
water lilies.

Don't look so intently, so closely.
Relax your mind.
Step back.
More of the picture will come
into view of your mind's eye.

*

Yes, i'm strange.
Deal with it.

You ask me how i am.
I respond, "Transcendentally magnificent!"

You wanted a default answer.
For your default mind.

*

There's a story i once heard
of the Dalai Lama.
He met the mother of a young girl,
who couldn't walk most of her life.
The mother begged him to help.
He leaned in and rested his
forehead upon the girl's cheek.
As he walked away,
the mother's eyes flowed with tears.

The girl's legs wiggled with freedom.

Do you believe in miracles?
They are truly everywhere.

So don't be afraid
to let me into your heart.
For, i am already inside you.
You breathe me. i am the air.

*

There was once a crumbling wall
that despite the army's efforts,
it simply could not be destroyed.

So i've been leaving you love notes
in every crack and crevice i can find.
One for every day that ever was
or ever will be in existence.

*

God rewards
the heavy-hearted
in this world
with
the lightest
conscience.

*

Last night, i had dinner
with my Father,
and a discussion unfolded
from him mentioning
the Kyaiktiyo Pagoda,
the Great Buddhist Golden Rock.

i spoke to him like Siddhartha.
He said i thought too much.

i love you deeply.

This bucket
has barely touched
the Waters in my Well.

*

Look closely.
Pay attention,
wherever you go.

The serpent's fang marks
are buried everywhere.

So i'm pressing my lips to everything
and sucking the poison out
of all the wounds.

i'm pressing my lips to You.

*

Live your dreams.
Chase the dress
through the forest

or immolate yourself
trying
trying
trying.

*

Irrespective of time,
we never have enough
when it comes to the ones
we love the most.

So focus your mind
on the here and now:

Cherish every beat
their Heart makes
when they are Near.

*

"What is the greatest gift
that you could ever bestow
upon someone?" i was
once asked. And i replied:

Kindness. Always, always Kindness.

"Why not love?"

Oh, silly.
Kindness is the *breath* of Love.

*

In space, there are black holes.
And theoretically their opposite, white holes.
People are also like these.

Some will suck the light out of you,
while others will pour light into you.

They believe light only escapes the white hole
and there is no way in.
But i have a secret if you're interested:
i can sneak you inside here, but shhh you must
be quiet. You can put your feet up
and relax a bit, i'll bathe you in
Light, and even show you the Source.

*

There's always that ageless
question: why would god allow
so many horrors and so much
suffering? i cannot speak for another,
but my simple thoughts are this:

To be the Greatest Parent,
you cannot baby your children.
This means letting them fall on
their face, or letting them get their
ass kicked out on the playground.
This brings terrible sadness to the
parent, but the wise know,
through struggle, all things grow.

And to be the Greatest Teacher,
it is more important to teach the
student freedom, to teach to
think for themselves...is this
not the most golden privilege
we so gracefully possess?

But don't get me wrong,
some things are so awful that even
i, in my trying to understand,
can't help but throw my Wine Glass against your Door.

But then the Clouds open up
like Heaven's Eyes,
and i watch the Rain come down
incessantly for weeks.
And that's when i know.
You feel *all* of our pain at once.

So i cup my hands and hold them
out and i Kiss your Tears,
because you taught me Simplicity.

It will be alright, my dearest dear.

*

i reiterate what the Buddha said:
Think for yourself, Question even
my words, do what works for you.

Because if a truth does not
resonate within you now,
maybe your vessel holds
different truths. Or maybe you
only see the silhouette of the
form now. But in time it will
begin to shift from formlessness
to form and you will recognize
the pattern, an echo from before.

*

Why get more bitter as you age?
Have you not been paying attention this entire time?

*

Please do not anger
my guardian and protector,
for She sleeps inside of me
and can be an awoken dragon.

When you continuously poke
me, i try and smile it off,
but she shows her teeth
through me. Her fangs dangle
from mine, and locusts
swarm, reaping inside
my mouth, while the bloodied nile
rises and overflows from my eyes.

i've seen grown men and women,
running for their lives.

But it's okay.
Shalom. Salaam. Shantih.
i only come in peace.
i only breathe love through my tree.

As-salamu alaykum,
All of my beautiful friends.

*

There's so much i don't Know
and even more that i Forget.
This Mind is like a Glacier
of Desolation, slowly melting
over time with the Sun's
Entropy, and so many vast
Crevices and Crags, where
my Ideas and Memories
slip away into Dark Abysses.

Such Freedom in Forgetting!

*

Beauty does not
require reciprocity.

Why do we believe
that love does?

Not to put a stick in your spokes,
since you're riding along
so adorably, but...

Why do we believe anything we do?
In what murky lotus'd mud waters
do any of these ideas *arise* from?

*

After my car accident and head injury,
i sat across a desk from a neurologist guru.

He said this:

"Do you know the mythology
of the mustard seed?
Focus your mind on nothing
but a mustard seed for just
5 minutes every day.
All your problems will dissipate."

In three casual sentences,
i gained more knowledge
than two decades of classrooms
could ever aspire to do.

*

i have no credit cards.
i see no point.

Why buy things
i do not need
with money
i do not have.

i am speaking literally
but also metaphysically.

*

What mad epistemology
is this, you say?
The world's going to end?
And such and such a date?

Well i must tell everyone...

Just kidding. Don't be a fool.
Don't tell such silly jokes.
There is no fucking end.
And if this material world
we believe to perceive
should unfold its atoms
back upon itself again or be torn to shreds,
don't fret. Us and billionfolds
of our progeny will have already
been returned to clay dust
and lifted into the wind
like fall leaves in autumn breezes,
back into the nighttime sky tree.

*

Oh my god, your Dress
and your Eyes like Olives at Night,
i remember them so intimately.
More clear than a Prophet's Vision.

Oh my god, your Love
stronger than the strongest Wine.
i am the Hummingbird blowing
you Kisses, my darling Trumpet Vine.

Come closer. Come near me.
i'll hold up the Sky's Mirror,
because there's nothing
as Beautiful as You!

*

Perhaps, it happened like this:

You stumbled home one evening
drunk and approached the wrong
Door. You thought it was your Home.
Silly Drunkenness! Yet, even when
you were realizing you weren't locked
out of your own home and instead
couldn't gain entrance to this new
home, you still Rang the Doorbell
and knocked softly upon the oak.
Perhaps, this was an accident.
Or, possibly it was the Friend
guiding you in your state to where
you truly have resided this entire time.
Thankfully, i was Home. And Awake,
patiently waiting for you to come to this holy home of
Ours.

So i came downstairs, Smiling
and i opened the Door and Kissed
you the first and last kiss of all
worlds that shall pass or come.

*

"Yousif, you stupid bastard
of a prophet. Why would you
ever leave the mountains,
knowing that only witch hunts
and persecutions would
follow you like swarms of hornets!?"

Simple. The Light of Love, carried
on a feather-painted songbird, led
me from my hiding to this world,
which is plagued by these
sufferings and injustices. Oh the
problems of man are created by
ignorant men and
nothing else beyond their minds.

Suffering all the horrors of the world
are but a cheap tax for Love & Beauty!

*

Dear Cern Supercollider,

Do you understand the Longing
that is induce by *separation*?
i am talking about the Mirror-Holder.
The One who's face i see in every
Star and Plant and Atom and Lake.

Our Great Mother, who we are all
more or less crawling back to.
Please, no more splitting & separating.
There is enough anguish & desolation
that the World's Heart knows too well.
If you can, put the pieces back
together, because that is inevitable
to the eternal recurrence of Form.

What is the Flute to do
without any of her Breath?
What is the Tree to do
without any Birds singing in her Hair?

What must any of us do,
knowing we've been split in two,
and that we are simply being
pulled back together from the pieces?

You may think a model like this
goes against conventional thinking,
concerning entropy. That the pot
that's pushed off the table and
breaks will never ascend back to
the table and be amended into One.

But i assure you, there are secrets
beyond our eyes and how we look,
where we miss the fact
that this Loving Madness
is happening all the time.

*

"What is that weird bulging
coming from you?" they ask me.
Ah, i am glad you ask because
it is for you and everyone
you know. It is the Great Mystical
Blanket of the entire universe.
In it, lined with Gemstones and Stars,
this Blanket holds all the power
and passion of living and dreaming
realities, of all possible outcomes,
and of all potential worlds. The Thread
which holds it all together is made
from the deepest love and compassion.

For these are what truly
hold our worlds, whole and individual,
all together forever. The Blanket contains every
idea ever thought and every feeling ever felt.
It is both freeing and eternally preserving for everyone.

"Why do you carry it with you?"
They asked me then.

Why else?
To wrap you all up!

*

Oh how the Whole Ocean
longed to woo that single
Raindrop, hiding in her Cloudbed!
There is much more contained
in your Eyes than the entire Night Sky,
and more Beauty pouring from
your Body than Sunlight in the Ruby.

Truth and Love are synonyms:

Like rivers, they continually evolve
with no end point, no conclusion.

*

Be neither surprised
not heartbroken
by the fickleness
of the human.
We are nature's
children in the end,
and She is ever
changing herself.
i feel those same
inner-currents, so
i can intimately relate.
However, i follow the
path of the sun,
the Great Lover
of Our Great Mother.

i am forever constant,
when she sways with
seasons and wind.
i am always there
for her to warm all
her soil for her growth
and to dry all of her tears.
And i won't be going anywhere.

*

Some seeds
are better
left buried
to find and
be exhumed
like Holy Bones
to be studied
at a much
later date.

*

There are no coincidences.
This thought arises from a doubt.
Let there be no more doubts!

A Cup overflows when it is filled.
Your Heart opens like a Garden
of Flowers with Rain and the Lights
you leave hanging over your
sleeping head. Crushed Grains
create the Bread. And when you
ask, it will surely come in some way.

Ask questions, but don't be questioning to what unfolds.
Empty your mind of selfish pride,
and humble yourself to what
slumbers deep inside. Observe,
even on your most simple
and uneventful days.

Assuredly, you can smell the Golden
Rose in an elegant pose:
it's always been hidden right under your nose.

Love, i've been leaving Breadcrumbs
for the trail you must walk,
letting them fall like Stars
and Pearls from my pocket.
Pick a few up when you need
them most and hold them close.
You will learn to sing along the way,
and you'll soon be the Bird perched
in its nest that awakens closed eyes
as the Sun comes up so eager to see You.

*

There's a difference
in the Shout
and the echo.
Most love the echo,
but the Shout *is* Love.

*

Sometimes the Tree overextends itself, trying to Shade the Flower, when the Winds or Rain are going to trample it into the ground. And in doing so, oftentimes the Tree's branches will break and end up crushing the Flower. Or in the Flower's position, sometimes she is focused so much on producing Pollen for her Bee Lover to the point that she herself refuses to Drink any Rain or Eat any Sunlight. This will only end in her poisoning the Bee and rotting in the Soil that will put all of the Garden in jeopardy.

Analyze these words deeply in love.
And promise to do neither of these.
Love and Nurture yourself as much as the Other,
enjoy Solitude and Space, then Cherish all you have.

*

Only the boldest of lover
has a heart strong enough
to bet on the unknown.
The Great Teacher says to
approach love and cooking
with reckless abandon.
This truth is like the sound
of Water dripping in my Cave
for all past time and time to come.
How could i not play this hand?
The Greatest Hand of Love?

*

i've only ever known
of colleges that give out
degrees in either drunkenness,
pretentiousness, or uselessness.
All real education comes from
experience, from nature,
and more deeply from within.

*

Everyone is a tied Knot.
Release yourself.

Everyone is a cracked Shell,
let your Seed Purse pour.

*

Inside and Outside,
i am entirely made of Flowers.

*

Our spiritual
and universal
wanderings
are the Coil
where we wind
and twist always
around each other
Spiraling freely
and continually
Connected.

*

Every thought you have, just know
that it's changing how you think, which
means it is changing who you are.

Remapping through elasticity.

i'm so confident in my lack of confidence.
So much love in my apathy.
So much growth in my wasting away.
So much living in all my dying.

All this Everything inside all this Nothing.

*

What a cowardly
and effete language.
The spun web of words
we tangle ourselves
and meaning in.

To be alone.
Literally "all one."
No one. is ever. *alone*.

As in: Solitary. By oneself.

We are all One.
ALL ONE,
we are.
Connected. And never
"Alone."

*

If you want Understanding,
look to Nature.
If you want Truth,
look within yourself.
If you want Love,
look to everything around.

It's all right *there*.
Here and now.

i hear the crosswalks,
making cardinal calls.

*

Be simple. Live simple.
Then life becomes simple.
i climb the Trees
and spend all day
lying around with the Birds.
i Sing out
between Pines,
Laughing
Songs to You.

*

Most people spend
their lives inside the House,
wondering what is on the other side
of several of the Doors.
Then the Doors are opened
and the same disappointments
and eruptions of joy unfold
by what those rooms hold:

All types of Happiness and Suffering,

Life Decay Love Sex Dancing Pain.

And yet most don't consider
that the House is temporary
and built by someone else.

And that there's so much more
simply outside those *walls*.

*

It is such a beautiful
relief to learn you've been wrong.
In this moment, the Flower opens
inside you and enlightenment comes.
To believe, but be shown otherwise,
is a great gift to receive.
It reminds you
how little you truly know.
So don't scoff with Heartache
at those Delightful Wings' flutter.
i am grateful that you came
and stayed up late Kissing me
while the neighbors
made Bread at 2am.
We giggled to Ourself.
Even though you said Nothing.
You said all there is to say.
You held me in those early
morning hours waiting to show
me the sun coming up
and the Birds singing your Songs.
Sometimes, that is the only reassurance we need.

*

Walking alone in the woods,
don't let the greediness
of your longing lead you.
Do not kick over the Stone
looking for your Other Soul.
Ask the Stone kindly.
It will Laugh to you and say
"*I* am who you've been looking for."
Then the Stone will turn to Dust.
And i swear, so will you.

*

i can only love.
But i cannot be
with the person
hidden in a shell.
i will moult you.
But i cannot stay
around anyone
living in total fear.
i'll kiss you and point
at the light, so you know where to run.
But i cannot stay.

Too many times have i
pulled the curtains back,
and someone is there
waiting for me with a knife.

*

We are completely absorbed
by sensations and desires.
Soaked in blood with wanting.
The Stars dangle
in darkened Skies
above over-thoughtful heads.
Empty yourself.
Push the Bowl off the Roof
in a Drunken frenzy.
Overturn a Table of Wine Glasses.
You reach for a Star
unable to grasp it.
Alter your perspective.
Love is never attained or possessed.
It is ever present.

FRIENDSHIP

*

Stop sad-heartedly
searching for Love.
Be It.

*

How long have I been
this *burning*
for the Friend of Friends?

*

Reverberating sigh,
rattling the trees,
shaking the earth's womb.

Another Tear falls
from my eye,
and turns into
a Rose as it hits
your page, Hafiz.

Oh, my brother,
you are never Alone!
Nor am i!

And neither are you,
all of my beautiful
friends!

*

If satan is real
and not just metaphor,
then i'll smother
my brother
in those holy Kisses,

cause i know
what it's like
to have such
a bad day as that.

But please don't
think that even
for a second,
after you've

been consumed
and moult your
bruised bones
to sand,

that our Great Mother
will not dust you off
and pick you up from
this earthly ground

to place you
back into
the Deepest Sky
of All.

*

Yes, just a bit
closer. A little
bit more. Ah,
perfect.

i needed to
see those
Jewels dancing
in your Eyes
once again,

because we
are all singing
the same song

as the whales
in the depths
of the sea

and the birds
with angel wings
fluttering day
and night
amongst the Fig Tree.

*

Use me,
dearest.
Please use
me for your
every whim
and need.

Take and take,
and take more.

Find me in
a dark alley
as the Speckled
Bird, blowing
kisses against
your wet Face.

My wells are
endless.

So i'll
always fill
you when you
get a little
empty.

*

In my recurring dream,
i am ravaging you,
delicately.
And You, ravaging me.

We are stripping the clothes
from one another
in a maddened frenzy.

You throw my glasses
to the hardwood floor,
where they break.
i toss your tossle cap
and untossle your hair.

Then the shirts.
The pants.
The underwear.

Finally, the socks.

We kiss.
And every moment becomes divine.

Because
i awaken
knowing…

We're stripping away our egos.
We're stripping away our insecurities.
We're stripping away past hurt.
We are deconstructing time.

We stand naked.
We unclothed our minds.

*

i have a crazy idea
(what is madness but genius
in an incomprehensible language?):

Would you like to become pen pals?

There's truly something of magic
in the feeling of ink-stained paper
sent across our Giant Circle.

It's okay if it's too much of a leap.

i'll still scribble Secrets
and sonnets
in the Stars
over your lovely Head.

*

Hug your friends.
Kiss your enemies.
Skip through dark
alleys laughing
while everyone is
asleep in the Silent
Dream so their
nightmares will
only be dreams
of Gardens forever.

*

Don't let
the Candle
Light
inside you
dim out.

Or i'll Kiss
your sad,
salty Face

and blow
the Flames
back
under the
Canopy
of your Heart.

*

Wake up!
My neighbor
of this house bed
realty we share.

i need to wipe
the sleep out
of your Kitten Eyes,

so you can see how
Beautiful everything
truly is today.

*

Kiss me
if you're a
Wilting
Flower,

and i'll
be your
Rain and
Sunlight

*

Lover,
i am spilling
Wine all over
your pages again.

Forgive me,
but i couldn't
go on any
longer without
everyone
knowing that our
Blood has merged.

And it flows through the same River
within the Heart of All,
where the cattail's
wiggle in the Light
alongside the banks
of Paradise's Lips.

*

Separated by
ten thousand Seas
and ten billions Stars,

a single incense
burning Light
deep in every realm
of the Trichiliocosm,

We dance.

Your hand
in mine.

*

i want to be
buried alive
within the chambers
of your Heart
and the prisons
of your Mind.

i'll build fires to keep warm.
i'll file down the metal bars.
And set us
both free.

*

Your mind is the most
Beautiful universe
for me to ever explore...

i promise to dust the Shelves

and place the Books
back where they belong

and kiss all those Paintings
hanging on the walls, then

i'll pull the curtains
to let the Light in.

*

Fall in love
with me.

i really mean *with* me.
Let's do it together.

Let's jump. Hold my hand.
Fuck the parachutes.

*

In the first star, we cuddled close.

Then: *separation*.

But i swam and swam.
i grew Bones for you.
i stood upright.
i climbed higher.

Through frozen Seas,
over new-formed Mountains,
and trampled Deserts,
i traveled.

My hair white,
My teeth fallen out,
i continued.

i died and grew again,
like perennials
on my own timeline.

Then,
finally...

Stars dimmed
and i recognized you
from across the Universe.

The same Stardust'd twinkle
in your Heaven Eyes:

My sweet,
my Cuddle Buddy.

*

i promise
i promise
my dearest
my sweetest Moon
to eat all your suffering
like a Flower
with sunbeams
stuck in
its Teeth.

*

You sit at the spinning wheel,
and Gold flows
from your Mouth
and from your Eyes.

You're a Songbird
on the banks of the Nile,
singing beautifully
as my Heart floods

washing away the past.
There, you'll find Stone
Tablets to unearth
from my Ancient Soil.

Lessons on how the crops grow.
Your Beauty is the only Truth i know.

But now, readjust your Lens
towards the Deepest Sky:
the Greatest Conjunction is coming.
i see the reflection in your eye.

*

There's no sense
in denying it:

We're fucking nuts.

Let me crack you open
and show you how
beautiful your
insides truly are.

*

Let me take your hand
and take you away from this world.

We can run through the Forest
and hide in a Tree fort with the Birds.

i'll Kiss you as many times
as there are Stars in the Universe.

*

It is a power
beyond knowing,
and my Heart
is splitting
all my Atoms.

What extrapolation
of such wonder
on how you make
even my bones hum
with the Universe.

*

Lie with me at the top of the world.

Teach me the names of all the Stars.

No, not what *they* call them.
Name them all yourself.

It'll be our little secret.

*

Don't let
yourself
be buried
alone
under cold soil.

Bury yourself
in my arms,
and i'll give you
Light and Love
forever.

*

You never have
to feel homeless,
because my Heart
is your forever Home.

You never have
to feel lost,
because my Love
is your Compass and Watch.

i carved your Name
on Heaven's Walls
and the Gates of Eden,
because i'll never
let you feel alone.

Now everyone knows
your Name and Loves you.

*

In the City of
Roses and Nightingales,
i will kiss you,
my little Moon Face,

until my Lips
are drunk with
the Wine
of your Love.

*

Little bird,
all i could ever want
is for you to land
on my shoulder
to rest
and to be my friend.

How long must i stand still and quiet,
letting you know
with only Heart and Breath
that you are safe with me?

*

True love
is unconditional
and all-encompassing.

i love the Flowers and the Trees
and all their Roots
and the deepest Soil

that has nourished them.
The bird's winged touch.
The honeybee's nuzzle.
The cloud's tears.
The solemn sun's kiss.

This is what makes all life grow,
so Lovely and Beautiful.

*

i'm sorry
so sorry
that i'm
not sorry
that i cannot
even focus
my divine
mind to
not gaze
upon
your
Beauty.

For, you are a perfect Pearl
at the bottom of a frozen lake.
And i cannot help wanting to rescue you,
and put you
in my pocket
to keep you
always safe.

*

Sister,
i've Kissed and Loved your Brother.

i found him lying on the roadside
with his Broken Wings.

i mended him and taught him to fly
back into your heaven nest,
where all the Trees grow eternal Fruit
and our Souls go to rest.

*

There is a Great Seed
within the cup
of your goddess Body.

And i, being the Water-bearer,
have been foolish most of my life,
drunkenly moving through this
existence, spilling wherever i go.

But i've sobered up. The Light
is shimmering through the water
now, as i water You completely.

We can Kiss to kill some time,
while that Seed blossoms
into Mystical and Magical things.

*

Fill me always
like an empty
teacup.

Crush me
like grapes
into Wine
to wet your mouth
and make
you drunk
off this Love.

*

How many men
have spoken Words
like mine to you?

How many men
have started so many
Fires in parts of you
you never knew
existed like me?

How many men
have offered to Kiss
all your Darkest Wounds
and Scars clean,
to plant you in new soil
like me?

How many men
have sung for you
through all the Rain
like a Songbird in
the giant Willow Tree
of your Soul like me?

How many men
have brought you
Treasures from other worlds,
laid them at your feet,
and built you Bowers
for protecting, asking
for Nothing in return like me?

How many men
have Loved every Atom
and Cell within the Temple
of your Holy Body like me?

How many men
have Watered the delicate
Seeds inside your Divine Mind
and your gorgeous Soul like me?

How many men
have Migrated their Souls
like Arctic Birds to live
in your Body as their
only Home like me?

i bet there are many!

But i am the Ocean
that lives inside of you.
Every bubble and every
particle of Salt in the Sea,
that's me! Vibrating to
the sleepy hum of your Heart.

My dear, i contain no Shoreline.
Never worry again!

i am ever expansive
and contain Everything in you.

My dear, you can float upon me
and Kiss my tired Lips
whenever you'd like.

*

i know your Mind
has been so heavy
like the Snow-covered
branches of the Great Pine.

Let me be your Sunlight.
i'll melt everything away
and lighten your load,
so your tender beautiful
branches may fully grow.

*

Why, my sweetest dear?
Why live in such fear?
Why let yourself
continually live
with Barren Crops
in this forever Drought?
Because i am the Rain Clouds,
just hanging out above you.
And let's be honest,
i've really got nothing going on.
Call to me, and i will drench you.
i will quench all the Unquenchable
deeply hidden inside of you!

*

Love can be a prison.
So choose your
Cell Mate carefully.
Both of you should
be recklessly in love.
Pick someone who
makes you Laugh
when darkness grips
your mind and blots your eyes.
Be yourself complete *alone*,
so you can be their true
counterpart and friend.
A Friend! Yes, pick someone
who is a goddamn friend
and a beautiful companion
to your mind and heart.
Pick someone who has
the Keys to the Cell
or knows how to pick locks!
And if all else fails,
pick someone who's at least
smart enough to sneak in
those metal files to wear
down the bars of your cell,
so you both can finally
go running, Naked and Pure
and Mad like true
Lovers under the Moon
and Sapped-Sycamores
toward your Holy Freedom!

*

i don't want to
ever Write
another thing

unless you
hang me
like a Dreamcatcher
to protect you
and all your Dreams.

*

The Sun gives Love
and Illumines the whole Sky,
but even if Clouds and Rain
happen to cover up all my blue,
remind yourself that i'll never
stop burning for You.

*

You know how to find me.
i've Painted all the Deserts
and left trails in the Stars. For you.
And those Flowers, over there...
they're whispering to you, of me.
Those Birds soar and sing overhead
and afoot, some of the things
that i have and must give to you.
But, yes. You know how to find me.
My Heart, my All,
will be here waiting,
if and whenever you want
for only ever You.

*

Sweetheart,
my love is a buried treasure.
i've burned all the maps.
i've broken all the keys.
i've disoriented the globe.
i've made the stars drunk.
i've covered all the tracks.
i've burnt all the bridges.
i've erased all the roads.
Because only You know where to dig.
Only You know the way in.

*

Invite me in.
i'll never take anything
from inside of you.
i won't ever disrespect
anything in your Palace.
i will build new Windows
and open locked Doors,
and create solidity, Freedom.
Because if you ever send me
away, you'll have all You need.

*

i want to watch you Bloom.
Soft and slow like a Pearl.
Hidden depths of a shell's mouth.
So beautifully foretold.
And if your Petals shall ever fall,
i'll be there to pick them up to put back in your Hair.

*

Dearest:

You deserve all things
filled with Love and Kindness
and Compassion. Let the
Flowers all Bloom in your
Heart and your Mind. Let
the Sunlight into your Garden
and even if there are Dark Clouds
and Rain, remember to rejoice
in them too, because they
are also Loving you deeply.

Sincerely,
A Representative of the Universe

*

i've annihilated my personal wants and desires.
i want to be a Friend to you, a Companion.
You entered my life like Lightning entering my Heart.
Now i sizzle. i am cooked meat.
No longer so Raw and Inedible.
For you, i only want to give.
To lift up and dust off, if/when needed.
And more than anything:
to cheer you on,
as you move with overwhelming
and Triumphant Beauty
through this Mystical life.

*

Why walk so
solemn and alone
when i am here
to take your Hand
and walk with you?

There's so much
Beauty i am able
to reveal before your Eyes.

*

The only love
i have to give you
is the Love
that's already
deep and overflowing
Oceans inside you.

i am your Mirror.
You are mine.

Look deep inside
the Water's Reflection
to hear me Laughing,
to see me Kissing you.

*

Francis, my brother.
When the earth took
you back to the Heavens,
all the Eagles flying
lost their Feathers
and they fell to blanket

the soft soil of your grave.
The Mountains wept
their icy eyes clean.
The Salmon stopped swimming.
The River went shallow.
The Coyotes ceased to howl.

We all just sat in meditation,
staring
at the Moon
looking for You.

*

Took an axe
to my Heart
and split it
like Firewood.
i only wish
that you were
here to share
this Beautiful
experience
with me.

*

My brother Crow's laughter.
The birdsong in your
Morning Heart.
And the half-crescent Moon
of the beautiful pregnant lady.
The sound of Stars falling
with the autumn Rain.
A mouth pressed

to the ground in praise.
All the Love that has
melted days into Daisies.

This is the Love
that the Friend
is always Giving.

*

Forlorn friend, Muhammad!
With weeping eyes, longing
for his brother Yusef's return.
The Planets are falling North
into the Caspian's womb.
How jejune are all written words
compared to the Silence of god?
Be not wearied.
Be free
like an unbridled Arabian horse.
My Love is in your every Breath,
within your every step.
You blink one million times a day,
and in your blindness,
i am there Kissing.
You cry out for my return.
Like all things, it is coming.
In the life of the Stars,
i've taken a forty year vigil,
waiting until the time is right
to become the Blood
that is making love
inside every Heart.

*

God is Silent.
There's so much Music.
We sit on a joined Star.
Together, holding hands.
Shhhh.
Listen.

*

A hole in the World
opens up.
i fall in.
You are there
waiting for me.
My mouth is too tired for talking.
Only kissing.

Read this poem aloud.
Feel me on your Lips.

*

Our first meeting:
i walked, searching
for a recognizable Face.
i see nothing but Eyes,
and the Universe moving
like an Ocean inside
and around them.
i faint.
i awake.
You are there holding me.
i say i've never fainted before.
i've never seen
anything so Beautiful!

*

Tomorrow and yesterday,
they are not my words,
but theirs, and i disbelieve.
How can you cut eternity
into small, manageable doses?
To me, there is only ever now.
And you are here,
Kissing my sleepy head.

*

Cry me a river.
i will drown you in it.
i've become the Ocean,
making love with the Moon,
my body moving
in tune with her.

Pranayama

i breathe inward
and swallow singing Birds.
i exhale,
Stars are spat dancing
into the Nighttime's Heaven Dress.

i've torn off all my Robes
and the Quilt covering your Eyes.
My Lips were Designed
to press against your Wounds.

LAUGHING

*

Have you ever
watched a Rainbow *die*?

*

The World's Greatest Lover
became a fool to Longing.
And whenever anyone,
even god,
started laughing at him,
he laughed with them too.
Because he *was* Laughter.

*

On such a sunny
day as this,
how many
Angels
are
tucking
their Wings
and doing
Cannonballs
off of the
Golden Gate
Bridge?

*

When was
the last
time you
simply
got Drunk
off the
Moonlight?

*

i'd like to explain
a bit of relativity
to you, if that
is alright.

How you see the Shooting Star
is different from the Star's Eyes.

Like Einstein's pebble
falling in a curved

parabola from the bosom
of the train,

i have fallen the same,
arching
ever more
into your Pocket.

*

Have you ever tasted the
Budding
Flowers
on your tongue
in the World's
most Heavenly
of Kisses?

*

There is never any Rhyme or Reason,
just a few Mystical seconds
right before the Volcanos
start to Dance...

*

How many
Scorpions
have i skipped
over in the Desert?

Lord knows!
Too many grains of sand to count,
and no matter!

Their Hearts are all happy
and singing to You and me.

*

Moonflower,
come beaming
to me
with your
Beautiful Lips
once more!

*

What will be
will be,
so i rest at ease.

*

You are the Flower,
and i am your Fragrance.
It is impossible for us
to exist without each other.

*

When the Heart speaks,
it only speaks Truth.

'Tis the mind
that fucking
befuddles
everything.

*

Have you
figured out
how friendly
my Mouth
is yet?

*

Just ask.

i'll take
all the Thorns
out quickly
and Kiss
the Wounds.

It won't hurt a bit. i swear.

*

Go have fun.
Go do whatever
the fuck you want.
Go be free,
truly free.

We're all going to Burn
like Gold some day anyways.

*

Never again.
Never,
will i misplace
my Precious Cup.

But please know
that you're all welcome
to come Drink from
this as much as you want.

*

Just lay with me
and tell me
all about your day.

i swear i'm more
interested in that
than how all
the Stars were born.

*

Poetry is meant
to be screamed
from the world's
rooftops
in a barbaric
yawp.
Sung like
bee kisses
into the lover's
heart, to give
to give
them wings

they never
knew
they had.

*

And the earth
will heat up
again with
your Love,
and all the
ice you thought
would stay
forever will
melt away,
and then you'll
skip through
the puddles
smiling like
the Child inside You.

*

i've so much
Love in my
life that i don't
know what to do
with it all.

So like the Madman
i am, i'll pack it up
in my suitcase
and flee the state,
Planting it all
along my way.

*

And what sort
of Divine Grace
could truly
encompass
all the Rain?

*

Dance
like the Moon
is in
your pants
and the
Stars
are caught
in your
lovely Hair.

*

My sweet,
did you know
the Birds sing
gallantly every
morning
in celebration
that you've Awoke?

*

My name is Cupid.
i bend my Bow for you.
i bend it for Love.

But sometimes,
i bend it
just for Fun.

*

i try not to
stretch too much.
i might accidentally
flick a Star from
the Sky
into your
Beautiful
Mouth
while you're
Smiling
at me.

*

At night, i am easily
and often awoken
by Angels softly
tapping on my Window,
begging me to come
out and cause some
Loving *mischief* with them.

*

Has the One replied?
i'm still staring into the Night Sky,
trying to study Her eyes.

*

The only thing
i ever get sad
about nowadays
is that i ever let
myself get
sad at all.

*

Roll around like
a playful child
in the ecstasy
of what others
shame you for!

What the fuck do they know?
Judging so, their lives must
be quite a bore.

Can you not
perceive god's humor?
It's sinister, i swear!
The Trees and i are
rattling and breaking
our Branches, laughing
this hard. Don't worry,
i'll tell you later.

*

You have me vibrating
at the sight of your Eyes.
But Silence now.

Eternal Silence.
i hear the Buddha
laughing boisterously
in your once
barren heart.
Oh, Heart like Mine!

*

So beautiful!
My half-mooned lover,
dancing naked
in the Violet
morning sky.

*

What do i know more
intimately than my own mind?
So many times
have you and i
played hide and seek.
i, often hoping
that you wouldn't find me.
But silly bastard me
to think for a second
you don't know all my hiding places.

You pull me out from under
the bed or behind the clothes
in the back of my closet,
and you hug me and kiss
my face like a puppy
after i return from a long day at work.

Silly bastard me, to try to
hide from all your love.
But c'est la vie,
from time to time.

*

Learn and practice patience.

What's the big
goddamn hurry?

Who wants
to rush
to die
anyways?

*

Let my love speak to you
most frankly and plainly:

Do not think too much.
Fret yourself even less!

What is our mind,
but a heap of organic
matter just bouncing
around in all this Space?

*

What is Hope?
The beautiful
boughs dripping

Fruit over the River,
while we bounce along
over the Rocks,
trying not to sink
too far below the surface.

*

i did not know you were
so High and Noble!

Here is a Truth for you:
just like the rest of us,
you breathe Tree Farts.

*

You are the only Star
in the daylight
of my forever mind.
No one can see you there,
Dancing and Beckoning
me with Kisses, but i do!
Oh my lord, you really are
my only lonely one, aren't you?

*

There are Beautiful Secrets
hidden beneath layers
of those Dark Universes.
My mind, in concentration,
can take me to the bottom
of all Oceans, where colorful
unnamed Fish float like Flowers

and spread their Love around me.
Remove your makeup
and empty your mind:
"Show me your original face
before your mother and father
were born."

*

Is there a point to all
of this evolution?
The way in which the
Watch begins working itself
and the Wheel continues moving?
The closed-eyed nihilist
would unheartedly disagree.

But what's any of it matter
to be truthful on the subject?

Have you tasted Lips that would
make the Sun go Blind?

Have you heard the Seeds in new soil
Singing and Dancing
just to feel the Rain's Touch?

*

We all end up
looking like idiots...
trying to kiss
the Moon.
But what else
are we supposed to do?

*

And then Another Day:
my Eyes are peeled open.
"Hey, asshole. Wake up!"
It's the Sun again.
It's beautiful outside, as always.
He wants me to come out
to play with Him and Her.
What a Divine Idea!

*

Have you gotten Drunk
off the Lips of my Love
recently?
Are you now alone,
Dancing with my Friend?

*

i used to only ever write
when i was uncontrollably sad.
But now i am so happy,
this Love is Bleeding
Everywhere
all over
our Pages.

*

A Prophet incapable
of
Predicting
himself.

*

How many Roses must
i pull from the Sea?
To build you the Shiraz
that you need.
To show a Flightless Bird
that it is truly Free.

*

And just as if the Joke were told
and actually heard this time,
the Sun conquered the grey Clouds
and broke into a Great Laughter.

*

The sadness breaks my Lung.
And you know the rest.
All of our Longing
is only a test.

*

New hobby:
limping in fractured foot luster.
How do you come and go
so quietly in the Nighttime?
As the Wax Moon hung
high above the Rose Garden
peeking in on her Children,
You were the Pearl buried under the Soil, just Laughing.
You were the Light buried under my Heart, just Singing.

*

i heard god Laughing
and watched a Dragonfly
fly into Her mouth
and an Ivory-billed
Woodpecker come flying out.

i heard god Singing
and my Mouth became
a Trumpet that sings
for only You.

i heard god Dancing
and i watched all
the Mountains rejoice and Smile
their White Teeth at the Sky.

i heard god Crying
and all the Rivers became full
and all the Plants grew.

i heard You whispering
to me in my Dream.
i couldn't make out the words.
But it was Truth i instinctively knew.

*

My fate is Drunk
again, Dancing with
the Stars
and i'm just
Humming
the Tune.

*

Heavenflower.
Yes, i've written to you before.
i have no intentions
to uproot you.
Or to pluck
your Petals off.
i will only Water
you and Shine
on you and blow
Kisses into your Lungs.

*

You grew like a Mushroom
in my Backyard for years.
Hidden from my sight.
Then your Spores flew
and scattered across this World.
Now i follow them to
re-piece you and me.
And my Heart is an Antiquated Chest
hidden in the Attic of your Soul.
A Secret within a Secret.
Hidden. and. Pure.
Coral reefs and Stones erode
and crumble into this Sea.
But all my songs are songs of You.
Open the box. Like a Heart.
i am here and always here.
The Treasure of your own
gorgeous Soul that's been
searching and floating
around this Perfect World.

*

Shake your Tambourine.
Rattle your Drum.
This Mystical Music
is for Everyone.
Only one message:
love. Love. LOVE.

*

Oh, your Heart is a Tree
and my Parachute
is caught in It!

*

How the fuck
am i not supposed
to find you
when you are Dancing
inside of me
Singing and Twirling
in Laughter
and Everyone
even the Trees
on these streets
are Smiling
with your Smile?

*

God throws Dirt in my Eyes
and runs away Laughing like a Child.

i ride toward the Sunset Smiling
and god puts a Stick in my Spokes.
i tumble over Stones, bloodied.

i stare at the Sun for days,
looking for your Face.
i see nothing but
blind phosphene spots
and trip over Myself everywhere.

What a playful
little
Cunt
You are.

*

Cry tears for the dead,
because they are Waking Up
and leaving our Dream behind
to Dance within the Light.

*

You opened your Parachute
inside my Heart.
Now i'll never fall
but gently with you,
and i'll always be Smiling
trying to find my way
out to Kiss your Mouth.

You opened your Parasol
inside of my Mind,
so now it never Rains

from those Grey Skies,
only through Sun
to make your Flowers
Inside of me grow.

*

We are all Love Dogs
barking at the door,
longing for our Owner
to return with our food.
They Nourish us, Love us.
And we pummel them
when the Door Keys
jingle outside.
We pounce with Love
and Infinite Kisses
never tiring of this
feeling.

*

The sun kissed me
so beautifully today
that i burn inside now.
Don't die on the toilet
like forgotten heroes,
you piss drunk fool!
Die in your bed.
Like an admirable champion
with a bottle of wine
on your night stand
with all your clothes on.
Alone.

*

i came here to Sing to the River.
To lie my Head in the Dirt
and weep for all the Lost Moons
that are left floating around
in Darkness searching for You.
i came here to fling Pearls
from the Oceans back into the Night
and to blow your dress up
that covers your Heart
like a heavy cloak
and to Kiss you like a Sleepy Bird
too tired for singing.
To call your Name
with both Eyes and Mouth closed
like a Rosebud on the Brim.

i came here to die.
i came here to give life.

When i was born,
they played a Sad Song.
When i pass on,
you'll point to the sun, Laughing.

*

i am sorry, Rumi.
i got too Drunk off
all your Laughing
and ate too many
Hallucinogenic Stars
i saw Dancing in the Night Sky.
i tripped over a Beam of Light

and fell Naked from above,
holding hands with the Moon.
We fell into your Well.
And the Water splashed
from my Cup into Yours,
and back again.

Every living poet
dies alone.

*

Are you Beautiful and Alone?
Then you are on the right path.
Are you dying inside the moan?
Then your Heart is a Bright Star.

Collapse, dissolve, die.
Become nothing,
to become everything.

The world is laughing.
The movement dancing in trees.
Remove *self* from reality.
Then the joke makes sense.

*

Only in the Drunkenness of such Music
do we learn to be Light.
So swift on our feet.
So shattered by Uncontrollable Smiling.

*

Come dance with me.
i love you.
i'm so Drunk i cannot see.
Only listening is here to guide me,
and your Soft Movements.
There is Presence everywhere
and it is overwhelming.
Through darkness, your Light
like Blue Flowers opening
inside of me.

*

i am a Weary Traveler
with broken hearts
lining my past
like tree ornaments.
You are a Gracious Host
who answers
when i wail and beat on your Door.
This Holy House is your Body,
and You're feeling kinky tonight.
You say:
"Friend, come inside me."
This is your Home now.

*

*

*

*

*

Wake up,
Sleepy Head!

i am your Dreams!

My Mouth is made
for more than just Poetry…

so

kiss

Me!

ABOUT THE AUTHOR

Józef Tracz-Ripple grew up in Pittsburgh, PA. He is author of the philosophy book, *Then Stirs the Feeling Infinite*, and the man behind the music project Józef Ripple & The Multiverse of Sound. Tracz-Ripple graduated from Robert Morris University in Moon Township, PA with a degree in English. He currently lives in Portland, OR.

www.ingramcontent.com/pod-product-compliance
Lightning Source LLC
Chambersburg PA
CBHW031441040426
42444CB00007B/925